THE HEALTHY CHURCH

practical ways to strengthen a church's heart

BOB WHITESEL

wesleyan
publishing
house

Indianapolis, Indiana

Copyright © 2013 by Bob Whitesel
Published by Wesleyan Publishing House
Indianapolis, Indiana 46250
Printed in the United States of America
ISBN: 978-0-89827-567-4

Library of Congress Cataloging-in-Publication Data

Whitesel, Bob.
 The healthy church : practical ways to strengthen a church's heart / Bob
Whitesel.
    pages cm
 Includes bibliographical references.
 ISBN 978-0-89827-567-4
 1. Church renewal. I. Title.
 BV600.3.W525 2013
 253--dc23
                        2012049802

To servant leaders seeking to strengthen
the heart of a church.
May this book in some small way add to your
effectiveness and impact.

CONTENTS

ACKNOWLEDGEMENTS

I am grateful to my colleagues, students, and clients who contributed their exercises and insights to this book. I am especially grateful to my colleagues in the field of church health and growth, including Drs. Eddie Gibbs, Gary L. McIntosh, Elmer Towns, Charles "Chip" Arn, Ryan Bolger, Kent Hunter, and Richard Peace. My colleagues at Wesley Seminary at Indiana Wesleyan University also provided indispensible insights, including Henry Smith, David Wright, Jerry Pattengale, Wayne Schmidt, Ken Schenck, Safiyah Fosua, Kwasi Kena, Colleen Derr, John Drury, Lenny Luchetti, and Joel Liechty. I am also grateful to this year's missional coaches, the budding church interventionists who I train each year in the practice of coaching churches: Jan Paron, Andrew King, and Joshua Henry. But the greatest support I receive is from my wife of thirty-eight years, Rebecca, and our family, Breanna, Mark, Kelly, Tory, Corrie, Dave, Ashley, and C. J., along with our lively grandchildren Kai, Cate, Abbey, and Capri. But most of all I am thankful to my Lord Jesus for leading me down this road of fascinating discovery into how churches can become the world-changers that he desires.

WHY CHURCH HEART HEALTH IS IMPORTANT

Heart-shattered lives ready for love don't
for a moment escape God's notice.

—Psalm 51:17 MSG

THE HEART OF THE MATTER

The Heart of St. Andrew

I thought I was the last to leave the room following the church council meeting. It had been a long and brutal evening, as fifteen aging and loyal leaders recalled with merriment and tears the eighty-year history of their congregation. "I guess we waited too long to do anything about it," came a soft voice from a darkened corner of the room. In the shadows, I saw Margaret, the pastor's wife.

St. Andrew Church was born in the early 1900s out of urban workers who immigrated to its factory town. Here they had forged a new life and faith community. But now the congregants had moved farther from the center of town, miles away from their urban church facility.

"I remember growing up in this church," Margaret continued. "It was full of life, full of love. But now it has the smell of death. Something happened over the years. The heart of our church just died. Programs replaced people. Pastors came, and once they had a little bit of success, they went. Most of our parishioners started coming just on Sundays. And fewer of us were left to do all the work. It was like a slow death. Our heart slowly got weaker. And now, I guess it's gone. You're too late Dr. Whitesel. We died years ago, and you're just here for the wake."[1]

And so began my desire to learn how to strengthen the emotional heart of a church. What actions could this church have taken to fend off the heart deterioration that seems to affect so many congregations today? And what are healthy churches doing differently to remain vibrant, flexible, and healthy as culture and communities change? As a researcher and consultant, I set out to learn the answer.

Out of thoughts swirling in my head that night came the seeds for this book. Over the next two years, I investigated churches that had survived and thrived in today's changing world. This book and its lessons are the result.

What Is the Heart of a Church?

The heart has long represented the place where emotions reside. As far back as Genesis, Moses described God as "heartbroken" over how his people had turned from him (Gen. 6:5–6 CEB).

Many other Scriptures (as well as poetry throughout the centuries) embrace the heart as a symbol of emotion.[2] Thus, the "heart of a church" will serve as a metaphor in this book for the emotions, passions, loves, and enthusiasms of a congregation.

From Where Does Congregational Heart Health Come?

God Notices Your Dilemma and Wants to Help. King David, no stranger to elation or despondency, sang about how God grieved when his children were brokenhearted: "Heart-shattered lives ready for love don't for a moment escape God's notice"

> The common church in America may be less than half the size it needs to be to attain effectiveness and health.

(Ps. 51:17 MSG). Since that is true, it doesn't escape God's notice or aid when congregation members' hearts are shattered over their church's health and future.

Starting Over. Earlier in the psalm, David hinted at the treatment: "God, make a fresh start in me" (5:10 MSG). Like David, many churches must seek to start over and recapture some of the health and heartfelt enthusiasm they once experienced.

It Takes Time. To the phrase "God, make a fresh start in me," David added, "shape a Genesis week from the chaos of my life" (5:10 MSG). The term *genesis week* carries the idea of starting over. A genesis indicates a beginning. When you combine *genesis* with *week*, the implication is that it will take time. It is not a genesis day or hour, but a judicious process. This book suggests one such process.

And so it is God—not programs, books, or curricula—that creates healthy emotions in a church's heart. This starting over begins with strengthening a congregation's heartfelt intimacy with God and then its positive impact upon others. But before we proceed, it must be understood that such health cannot be manufactured or artificially conceived. Heart health starts by deepening a congregation's experience with God. And in response God creates a fresh start that creates a new heart out of the common chaos of congregational life.

THE UNCOMMON CHURCH

What Is the Difference Between a Common and Uncommon Church?

It is common for churches to be in chaos, suffering from a congregational heart that is exhausted, ailing, and even barely functioning. For example, today the common church is attended by only about seventy-five people,[3] but experience has led me to believe the minimum number of attendees should be around 175 if the church is to function effectively. That means that today the common church in America may be less than half the size it needs to be to reach effectiveness and health. This puts a great deal of strain on the leaders of a church and the church's heart.

> A whopping 82 percent of Americans do not regularly attend any church.

With the common church in such a state of ill health, many people avoid it. Recent studies suggest that only about 18 percent of Americans actually attend church regularly.[4] That means a whopping 82 percent of Americans *do not* regularly attend any church.

As a result, there is sizable segments of America to which churches can reach out, but most churches are too weak and too emotionally frail to do so. This heart-shattered church, in need of closeness to God and passion for his offspring, may be alienating sizable segments of the nonchurchgoer population. The heart-shattered church may just be the most common church in America.

What Does the Uncommon Church Look Like?

A church that remains spiritually vibrant over many years, with intimacy with God and ministry impact, appears uncommon today. Still, uncommon churches are out there. I have come across many that enjoy long-term intimacy (with God and each other) and long-term impact (in reconnecting people to their loving heavenly Father[5] and to one another). The key is to learn what they are doing to maintain their congregational heart health.[6]

> The key is to learn from uncommon churches what they are doing to maintain their congregational heart health.

So what would it take to buck the trend toward commonality? What would it require for churches to start fresh and have a new beginning from the chaos of church life? And what would it look like if a new strategy brought churches closer to God and empowered them to have more impact in their communities? It is toward helping churches attain an uncommon health, growth, and partnership with God's mission that this book is dedicated.

ONE

THE KEY

A WONDER TREATMENT

Imagine that a new wonder drug has been created. It will help prevent
illness and disease . . . [and] help you lose excess weight—and keep it off.
It will slow the aging process . . . give you energy and increase your
self-esteem . . . reduce stress, fight depression and anxiety. . . .
Now imagine that this drug doesn't cost a penny.

—Mayo Clinic

THE TREATMENT BEGINS WITH SEEING THE CHURCH AS A BODY

The Church Functions Like a Human Body

For good reason, the New Testament writers often compared
the growing, interrelated, and complex nature of the church to a
human body. Writers such as Paul felt readers could better grasp
what God wanted for the church by envisioning the church as a
human body (see figure 1.1).

Figure 1.1

THE CHURCH AS A BODY		(emphasis added)
The church functions like a human body.	Romans 12:4–5 MSG	"In this way we are like the various parts of a human *body*. Each part gets its meaning from the *body* as a whole, not the other way around. The *body* we're talking about is *Christ's body* of chosen people. Each of us finds our meaning and function as a part of his *body*."
	1 Corinthians 12:12 MSG	"You can easily enough see how this kind of thing works by looking no further than your own *body*. Your *body* has many parts— limbs, organs, cells—but no matter how many parts you can name, you're still one *body*."
	Ephesians 4:25 MSG	"No more lies, no more pretense. Tell your neighbor the truth. In *Christ's body* we're all connected to each other, after all. When you lie to others, you end up lying to yourself."
The church can be built like a body.	Ephesians 4:12 CEB	"His purpose was to equip God's people for the work of serving and building up the *body* of Christ."

But the Church Is Also Christ's Body

Even more remarkably, the New Testament writers saw the church as analogous to Christ's body. They sought to help a struggling yet growing church understand it was not just any body, but Christ's body of testimony, life, and power upon the earth. New Testament writers also reminded the church that just as a body needs nourishment, the church also needs to get its strength from God (see figure 1.2).

Figure 1.2

THE CHURCH IS CHRIST'S BODY (emphasis added)		
The church is Christ's bodily presence on the earth.	Ephesians 1:23 MSG	"The church is *Christ's body*, in which he speaks and acts, by which he fills everything with his presence."
Spirit-empowered leaders lead this body.	Ephesians 4:11–13 MSG	"He handed out gifts of apostle, prophet, evangelist, and pastor-teacher to train Christ's followers in skilled servant work, working within *Christ's body*, the church, until we're all moving rhythmically and easily with each other."
Christ is the head and nourishes this body.	Colossians 2:19 MSG	"He is the Head and we are the *body*. We can grow up healthy in God only as he nourishes us."
The Holy Spirit nourishes the body.	1 Corinthians 12:13 MSG	"Each of us is now a part of his resurrection *body*, refreshed and sustained at one fountain—his Spirit—where we all come to drink."
Do not forget this analogy.	1 Corinthians 12:27 MSG	"You are *Christ's body*—that's who you are! You must never forget this."

The Wonder Treatment the Mayo Clinic Discovered

Since the writers to the early church used bodily analogies to explain church principles of leadership, presence, unity, and variety, then it would seem fitting this analogy could be extended to the health of the church as well.[1] Fuller Seminary's professor emeritus of church growth, Eddie Gibbs, once said, "Churches like people have died, because they refused treatment until it was too late."[2] Let's look at what wonder treatment researchers at the Mayo Clinic have uncovered. Notice its parallels with the church:

Imagine that a new wonder drug has been created. It will help prevent illness and disease . . . [and] help you lose excess weight—and keep it off. It will slow the aging process . . . give you energy and increase your self-esteem . . . reduce stress, fight depression and anxiety, and put you in a better mood. It will make you stronger and healthier. . . . Now imagine that this drug doesn't cost a penny. . . . This miracle drug is available right now—and you can start taking it today. It's called exercise.[3]

What Motivates People to Exercise

With such a wonder drug available, why is America so infamously flabby? The answer lies in three reasons why people don't regularly exercise. And for the wonder treatment (exercises) in this book to be profitable, such exercise excuses must be addressed.

People Will Exercise if the Exercises Are Right for Them. Exercise becomes enjoyable when a person finds an exercise that is right for his or her age, health, and interests.[4] But most people fail to find suitable exercises because they don't know the wonderful variety that is available. This book will describe many exercises that can be the starting places for finding heart-strengthening exercises that are right for your church.

> With such a wonder drug available, why is America so infamously flabby?

People Will Exercise if the Exercises Are Productive. Everyone knows that exercise with little result is not very inspiring or motivating. Therefore, the exercises in this book have been taken from colleagues, researchers, students, and case studies to suggest exercises that yield real-world results.

People Will Exercise if the Exercises Are Fun. Exercise that is enjoyable is more likely to be repeated. Once people or churches find exercises that are pleasant and enjoyable for them, they are likely to repeat them. The exercises in this book were selected not only because they are effective, but also because they incorporate enjoyable and fun congregational activities.

When the right exercises are discovered, when they are enjoyable to undertake, and when positive results are forthcoming, churches will exercise. This book investigates varying congregational exercises and the principles behind each so that the heart-shattered church can begin a treatment that will lead to health.

A CAVEAT: NOT ALL EXERCISE IS BENEFICIAL

Sometimes people hesitate at this point, recalling the King James admonition that "bodily exercise profiteth little" (1 Tim. 4:8 KJV). There is truth here. Bodily exercise—if done for the wrong reasons and in the wrong manner—will not achieve what God desires for a human body or for his church. So before we progress further, let's look at two potentially harmful outcomes of exercising in the wrong manner.

Overdoing It
Everyone is aware of athletes who have pushed their bodies too far with deforming results. The same can be true of the exercises in this book. Some congregations focus so much on such exercises (and repeating them) that they forget the goal of their exercising. Just think about how churches conduct annual rallies, block parties, revivals, and other such events that have outlived their relevance to strengthening a church's intimacy with God and impact on others. To offset this misstep, we will see that the

exercises in the following pages are neither the purpose nor the focus of this book. The mission of this book is something more eternal than physical or spiritual calisthenics. The purpose of this book is exemplified in the opening story drawn from a compilation of client interactions. The objective of this book is to help churches develop a carefully thought-out and appropriate exercise regimen that will increase the effectiveness of the church's ministry, deepen its intimacy with God, and as a bonus, increase the church's longevity.

Overconfidence

The media has made us aware of those who exercise their bodies for selfish rationale and arrogance. The church can succumb to similar pressures. I have written elsewhere how churches often become overly confident or intoxicated with their growth to the point of hubris and ruination.[5] The most important thing to remember is that an exercise treatment must have a proper goal. Exercise that is undertaken for vain self-satisfaction will often mirror that vanity in disfigurement and deformity.

> Exercise that is undertaken for vain self-satisfaction will often mirror that vanity in disfigurement and deformity.

To guard against church exercise becoming the focal point, let us take a brief look at God's purpose for church exercise.

BUILDING HEALTHY HEARTS FOR THE RIGHT REASONS

When 1 Timothy 4:8–9 is considered in a modern translation, a more robust admonition emerges: "Exercise daily in God—no spiritual flabbiness, please! Workouts in the gymnasium are useful, but a disciplined life in God is far more so, making you fit both today and forever. You can count on this. Take it to heart" (MSG).

Do you as a church (and individually) want to be "fit both today and forever"? You can be. But it begins with the right reasons: *impact* and *intimacy*. Let's explore each.

Impact: Perkins's Three Rs

Almost everyone today agrees that churches should make a positive impact in their communities. But how do we measure such impact in today's socially and spiritually divided world? I find the insights of John Perkins particularly helpful. Perkins was born in the segregated South of the 1930s. He ran away to California after his brother was shot by a policeman. Still, he couldn't run from the One who pursued him. In California John Perkins met Christ, who compelled him to return to his native South. There Perkins set up urban cooperatives to share food, clothing, child care, medical facilities, and most importantly, Bible studies where attendees were given the opportunity to experience Christ's salvation which had so profoundly changed Perkins.[6] In response to his spiritual transformation,[7] Perkins urged healthy churches to impact their world through what he called the three Rs.[8]

Redistribution. Perkins envisioned wealthy suburban churches not having lavish facilities, expensive decorations, and marble floors, and instead sending money to inner-city churches that were meeting the needs of the poor. He knew that per capita giving in urban churches was far below the surplus income that suburban churches enjoy. He envisioned the wealth of the middle-class churches being voluntarily and sacrificially shared with lower-income churches so that both churches could make a bigger impact. Far from an imposed redistribution of wealth, John

Perkins saw the church willingly and joyfully avoiding lavish spending in order to give more money to congregations that were making a difference among people of meager incomes.[9]

Relocation. Perkins also envisioned suburban churches that had left urban areas returning to deploy their volunteers into impoverished areas.[10] Churches could plant indigenous venues and ministries in urban areas, then raise up local leaders to lead them. Rather than leaving the urban struggle behind when they moved to the suburbs, Perkins envisioned suburban churches returning with viable and effective need-meeting ministries for urban locales.

John Perkins envisioned the wealth of the upper-class churches being voluntarily and sacrificially shared with lower-income churches so that both churches could make a bigger impact.

Reconciliation. The most important R was reconciliation, both physical and spiritual.

- Interpersonal (Physical) Reconciliation. Across the social, ethnic, and economic divides that segregate a country, Perkins saw churches comprised of diverse cultures, working shoulder to shoulder. Perkins envisioned every church involved in cross-cultural partnerships and modeling the church of Revelation 7:9, where "Everyone was there—all nations and tribes, all races and languages" (MSG). What better way to prepare for the montage of peoples pictured in that verse than for the church to start to approximate that mosaic in its partnerships and its makeup?
- Spiritual Reconciliation. Perkins knew that it was not social reconciliation that was God's endgame. God desires a more supernatural and eternal reconciliation. Perkins envisioned

churches as welcoming and nurturing salvation experiences. This was the ultimate reconciliation that only God could provide through his Son, and verses such as Romans 5:10 and 2 Corinthians 5:18 remind us of this.

Impact Exercises. The following chapters are packed with impact ideas, illustrations, and discussion starters that can help bring about the three Rs (and most importantly spiritual reconciliation) through the work of a local church. But the power for such exercise must come from somewhere. That strength can only arise from a deepening *intimacy* with our heavenly Father.

Intimacy: Prayer, Meditation, and Communion with God

Because the church has been given such a life-altering and world-changing ministry of reconciliation, it discharges its duties best if done in unity and grace.

Supernatural Unity. Regrettably, most readers have encountered churches filled with strife, petty disagreements, and social rifts. Yet it was Jesus' wish for his church to demonstrate a supernatural unity that amazes a watching world. Jesus said, "I'm not praying only for them but also for those who believe in me because of their word. I pray they will be one, Father, just as you are in me and I am in you. I pray that they also will be in us, so that the world will believe that you sent me" (John 17:20–21 CEB).

Many things are striking about this passage, but two stand out for our present concern. First, Jesus willed that the church would be as united and harmonious as he and the Father. This was, in part, so a watching world would believe their message. Second, Jesus prayed that the church would be "in us," suggesting that such harmony emerges out of intimacy, closeness, and connection to God.

Jesus' prayer began to bear fruit in the early church which had been divided by religion, ethnicity, status, and tradition. The early church began what can only be described as a great journey toward cross-cultural integration, wrestling with ideas about tradition (Acts 11), outward signs of godliness (Rom. 2), and estranged cultures (Acts 15). The emerging dissonant harmony allowed the church to have an expanding impact upon its neighbors. Early church historian Tertullian famously said, "What marks us in the eyes of our enemies is our loving kindness. 'Only look,' they say, 'look how they love one another.'"[11]

Intimacy Exercises. One purpose of the exercises in this book is to bring churches and individual Christians into a healthier relationship with God for greater intimacy. Each exercise list begins with intimacy ideas designed to bring the reader closer to God. Of all of the exercises in this book, these exercises of personal, spiritual health should be performed first. To undertake any church health regimen without attention to strengthening spiritual health would be fruitless. If the harried reader finds that he or she lacks time to fully digest the exercises in each chapter, I recommend that the personal intimacy exercises be your priority. Congregational health can emerge from the proper mental and emotional attitudes of the congregants, but the reverse usually never occurs.

AN OVERVIEW OF THE EXERCISES IN THIS BOOK

The following chapters are divided into seven exercise topics and a final chapter on how to make these exercises relevant, enjoyable, and productive. Each chapter offers exercises that people and congregations have utilized to maintain heart health and vibrancy. As noted above, the first exercises in each list will deal with developing intimacy with God, which undergirds and creates the impact of the exercises that follow.

Chapter 2 examines how the church experience creates a closeness that fosters accountability, interdependence, and camaraderie. But a clannishness can also occur, fostering division and separateness. These exercises will foster both unity and purpose.

Chapter 3 tells of the church providing a unique haven and refuge for hurting people. This means that a church will always have hurting and damaged people coming into it. Taking care of these damaged people requires the church to practice exercises that create a safe environment where love, acceptance, and empowerment encourage people to overcome their ailments.

Chapter 4 discusses how today's growing mosaic of cultures (ethnic, generational, affinity-based, etc.) means today's society is constantly more fractured. These exercises strengthen a church's ability to bring together, unite, and reconcile diverse cultures.

Chapter 5 provides exercises that can create team building, acceptance, and accountable discipleship with insights drawn from John Wesley's band meetings. This will not only broaden the leadership base of a church, but also develop moral responsibility and discipleship.

Chapter 6 will help churches avoid the Sunday morning performance trap and instead create authentic worship experiences where encountering God becomes the focus.

Chapter 7 discusses how ever-increasing globalization requires the church to be the hands of Jesus Christ both locally and globally. But at the same time, the church must not forget its duty to strengthen congregants. A new term, *conglocal*, will be proposed and explained to help churches remember the three-fold emphasis on meeting congregational, local, and global needs. The exercises in this chapter will foster Christlike living both within the congregation and in cross-cultural ministry locally and abroad.

Chapter 8 will help a church understand and foster the spiritual transformation that comes from a personal relationship with Jesus. These exercises will assist congregations in developing an environment where spiritual transformation is expected and central.

Chapter 9 may be one of the most important, for here you will discover how to adapt and modify the exercises to your specific church situation. By following three principles of customization (called *improvisation*) you will learn how to adapt the best aspects of an exercise or even combine multiple exercises to create a heart-strengthening regimen for your church.

ARE YOU READY TO BEGIN?
THERE IS NO TIME TO WASTE!

Are you ready to explore exercises that can prevent your church from decline, weakness, and irrelevance? The exercises in this book fulfill the three elements for a successful treatment. First, they are flexible so that they can be customized, combined, or adapted to find an exercise that is right for your church. Second, they can produce intimacy and impact in churches of varying size, denominations, and locales. And third, in addition to leading to health and relevance, many of the exercises will be so enjoyable that your church will want to repeat them.

Don't let anything stop you now. Delve into the following pages with your church leaders, and you will find a treasure trove of creative, enjoyable, and spiritually healthy ideas that will increase the longevity, vibrancy, impact, and intimacy of your church.

QUESTIONS FOR REFLECTION

1. How do you feel about physical exercise? Do you practice it regularly? Have you in the past? What are the current results, and what do you wish you could do differently?

2. Does your church try new things, such as spiritual and ministry exercises to stretch itself and improve its health? What are the current results, and what do you wish you could do differently?

3. Where are you in your spiritual journey: stuck, moving ahead, slipping behind, or somewhere in-between? How is your intimacy with your heavenly Father? When have you been close to him in the past? And could you return there again? What will you do tomorrow to maintain or regain that closeness?

4. How have you been a force for reconciliation between people with strong disagreements? When have you been a force for reconciliation in the past? Could you recreate that again? What will you do tomorrow to better participate in a ministry of reconciliation between people?

5. How have you been a force for reconciliation between people and their heavenly Father? When have you been a force for reconciliation in the past? Could you recreate that again? What will you do tomorrow to better participate in a ministry of spiritual reconciliation between someone you know and their heavenly Father?

TWO

THE CHURCH AS A TRIBE

EXERCISES FOR UNITY

The goal is for all of them to become one heart and mind—
just as you, Father, are in me and I in you.

—John 17:21 MSG

DOWN THE STREET IN ANDERSONVILLE

Look Different

"The church is supposed to look different, a place for forgiveness, acceptance, and harmony. Isn't that the thing?" began Caleb, a trustee of Andersonville Community Church. "Well maybe we did once, but no more." And so I was welcomed back to this growing church on the edge of town. I had been hired to help it deal with its newfound growth, but as I came to know the congregation better, I saw the growth had not led to harmony. Actually, it had the opposite effect.

"We're squabbling about so many things," continued Caleb. "If it wasn't for our strong Sunday schools and programs for the needy, I don't think anyone would even be interested in coming here. We're doing so many good things and people are coming here because of it. But a good ministry can't compensate for a lousy fellowship environment. Good thing you are here. It's getting worse."

Too often the common church is weighed down with division, petty squabbles, and power struggles. This even happens in churches that on the outside seem to be doing fine. And the problem is complicated when spiritual inquirers visit our congregations seeking solace and aid but only find more squabbling.

It is not surprising that Paul reminded the Ephesians how important it was for the church to reflect a different kind of environment than the world exhibited: "And so I insist—and God backs me up on this—that there be no going along with the crowd, the empty-headed, mindless crowd. . . . You learned Christ! . . . What this adds up to, then, is this: no more lies, no more pretense. . . . Make a clean break with all cutting, backbiting, profane talk. Be gentle with one another, sensitive. Forgive one another as quickly and thoroughly as God in Christ forgave you" (Eph. 4:17, 20, 25, 31–32 MSG).

Look Like a Tribe

There are many ways to describe the church: a fellowship, a congregation, and a community. But I've noticed a refreshing alternative among those who lead young churches. To them, terms like *fellowship* and *community* seem too associated with a complex organizational structure. Instead, they often use a word borrowed from the developing world: *tribe*. At a church called Tribe of Los Angeles, a young attendee described it this way:

"Tribe tells people we are doing something different at church. It means we are close, like a family. And it also says we are in this together, that we are small but mobile, that we have a closely held, common task. It's just like a tribe in the developing world that must work together to survive."[1]

I find something refreshing in terms that sum up a family-like dependence. Now I am not recommending that churches adopt such terminology to appear relevant. But I find that using *tribe* on occasion reminds us all that the church is on a mission and the accomplishment of that mission depends on the church being a mutually supportive team.

THE POWER OF UNITY

Fulfilling Jesus' Prayer

In John 17:21–23, Jesus prayed that all believers throughout all time would demonstrate a supernatural unity. And he stressed that this unity would amaze the world: "The goal is for all of them to become one heart and mind—just as you, Father, are in me and I in you, so they might be one heart and mind with us. . . . Then they'll be mature in this oneness, and give the godless world evidence that you've sent me and loved them in the same way you've loved me" (MSG).

Such a passionate desire from the Son of God cannot be dismissed easily. But this was more than just a longing. Jesus emphasized a purpose in this unity when he stated, "Then they'll be mature in this oneness, and give the godless world evidence that you've sent me and loved them" (17:23 MSG).

Unity Supports God's Mission

God's mission (sometimes called the *missio Dei*) is that he wants to reunite with his wayward offspring. Jesus made it clear that only through his sacrifice was this reconciliation possible (John 14:6–7; Rom. 3:23–24; 5:8; 6:23). And though the church supports this mission in many ways, there are least three important ways that church unity contributes to reconnecting people with their heavenly Father.[2]

Community Influence. Jesus wanted his church to be so loving, forgiving, and united that the secular world would take notice. He desired the evidence of this amazement to not be theatrics, but evidence that God sent him and loves all people (see John 17:23). When a church is uncommonly united, this contrasts with the disunity found in most worldly organizations. It reminds the watching world that something supernatural is at work in our churches,[3] and it models to the world the undivided nature of God.[4]

Cross-Denominational Influence. Church leaders often influence other congregations by packaging innovative programs and selling them as growth inducers to other congregations. But too often these are tactical programs that may work only for a short time. Churches that latch onto such tactical programs often adopt tactical names, such as seeker-friendly churches, cell churches, missional churches, body-life churches, or Samaritan churches. But, as seen in Jesus' prayer, it might be more fitting for networks of churches to be known for their unity more than their innovations.[5] Congregations that are united can model important attributes of forgiveness, harmony, and agreement that the secular world finds hard to muster.[6]

Congregational Influence. A united congregation provides an environment where congregants can spend more time, energy, and focus on the needs of those outside of the organization, rather than scrutinizing the differences of those within. I often observe churches so focused on their internal squabbles that they miss (and usually repel) visitors and seekers who God is sending their way. But when churches

> The secular realm can be a place of antagonism, bitterness, and factions. It is no wonder that weary souls worn down by this often search for an environment where divisiveness is minimal. Many hope to find this harbor in Christ's church.

become more united, they recycle more time and energy into the dire problems of those not yet reunited with their heavenly Father.

Nonchurchgoer Influence. The secular realm can be a place of antagonism, bitterness, and factions. It is no wonder that weary souls worn down by this often search for an environment where divisiveness is minimal. Many hope to find this harbor in Christ's church. If they instead encounter false compassion and hypocritical jockeying for influence, they can easily conclude that the church is hypocritical, promising solace but only offering hostility. As Paul noted, a united, loving, and forgiving church means "no going along with the crowd, the empty-headed, mindless crowd" (Eph. 4:17 MSG).

A Caveat: Dissonant Harmony

The above reminds us that the church must regularly seek to strengthen its unity in the presence of a disunited world. But is unity really attainable? The clear answer is that perfect unity is not achievable, at least not in this earthly realm. Scripture reminds us: "There's nothing wrong with God; the wrong is in *you*. Your wrongheaded lives caused the split between you and God. Your sins got between you so that he doesn't hear" (Isa. 59:1–2 MSG);

"For all have sinned and fall short of the glory of God" (Rom. 3:23); and "If we claim that we're free of sin, we're only fooling ourselves. A claim like that is errant nonsense" (1 John 1:8 MSG). Therefore, no church can attain perfect unity when fallible human beings are involved.

Instead, the church should strive, with God's help, to be increasingly united. The goal is not *perfect* unity, but *more* unity. Two colleagues of mine label this as "dissonant harmony."[7] By this they mean that a church can never attain perfect harmony, but it can attain a degree of harmony that is increasingly harmonious, acknowledging some dissonance and dissension. Christ's prayer is not that churches fabricate mindless slaves to corporate vision. Rather, Jesus emphasized that church unity was to be an earthly reflection of the miraculous oneness amid diversity of the Trinity. Striving to be more unified has benefits that make the effort worth it. And besides, it is the Master's prayer.

> Christ's prayer is not that churches fabricate mindless slaves to corporate vision. Rather, Jesus emphasized that church unity was to be an earthly reflection of the miraculous unity amid diversity of the Trinity.

EXERCISES FOR UNITY

Unity in My Church's History (Intimacy)

Exercise Plan. Write a historical analysis of your church (as far back as you can go; fifteen years at most). Answer these questions: When has your church been unified? When has it been divided? What was going on that caused your church to be unified or divided at those times? Based on your answers, what could you do to foster more times of unity in the future?

Variations. This exercise can be applied to small groups such as a Sunday school class, worship team, or leaders' retreat.

Principles. Looking back on how God has worked in the lives of churches as well as in the personal lives of Christians can help us become aware of the Holy Spirit's work. Conducting a semi-regular evaluation of the times when God united your congregation can make it easier to anticipate how and when God will move in this manner again.

Unity in the Midst of Dissonant Harmony (Intimacy)

Exercise Plan. Write one paragraph describing what dissonant harmony means to you. Then underneath that paragraph write your answers to the following questions: Can people work together and accomplish goals while still not being in perfect agreement? What are some historical examples of dissonant harmony in your life, the life of your church, or the history of your nation? What do the above exercises tell you about the meaning of dissonant harmony?

Variations. You can also use this exercise to evaluate a ministry, relationship, or occupation. While varying the topic, the key is to look back at times that may have appeared idyllic, but actually included quite a bit of tension.

Principles. In hindsight, the past may appear wonderful, when in reality those times may not have been as harmonious as we remember. This exercise helps us see that conflict will always be present to some degree.

Unity in the Midst of Struggles (Intimacy)

Exercise Plan. Write one paragraph describing what you think Paul meant when he said, "Most important, live together in a manner worthy of Christ's gospel. . . . Do this so that you stand firm, united in one spirit and mind as you struggle together to remain faithful to the gospel" (Phil. 1:27 CEB). Then answer the following questions: What does this passage mean to you when it says Christians should "stand firm, united in one spirit and mind"? And, what is the struggle it is referring to when it says "as you struggle together to remain faithful to the gospel"?

Give two examples of struggles you have encountered in which you found it difficult to maintain unity with others. Now, write out a plan regarding what you will do in the future to handle struggles "in a manner worthy of Christ's gospel."

Variations. If you are a pastor or paid employee, you might want to apply this to your ministerial work environment. This can be eye opening. Another variation is to apply this to your family setting, to see to what degree your relationship with those closest to you has been an example of Christlike living.

Principles. This exercise helps us see that though there have always been times of discord, we usually manage to work through these struggles with God's assistance. Disagreement is a part of life, but handling it in a manner worthy of Christ's gospel requires effort and prayer.

Unity in the Midst of Diversity (Impact)

Submitted by Gary L. McIntosh, professor of Christian ministry and leadership, Talbot School of Theology, Biola University, La Mirada, California.

Exercise Plan. At a church fellowship gathering, have people stand and move around as the leader gives the following directions.

First say, "If you've been attending this church for fewer than five years, stand on this side of the room. If you've been attending for six years or more, stand on the other side of the room."

Then ask each person to quickly share with their group his or her name and how they first heard about the church. Keep it short.

Next say, "If this is your first time to attend a fellowship event at our church, stand in this corner. If you've been at a fellowship event before, stand in this corner." Then ask the first time people to share with their group their name and tell how they came to the event.

Then say, "If you have children still living at home, stand on this side of the room. If you don't have children living at home, stand on the other side of the room." Then ask those who still have children living at home to tell how many children they have.

Finally say, "If you live within five miles of the church building, stand in this corner. If you live six to ten miles away, stand in this other corner. If you live eleven to fifteen miles away, stand in that corner. And if you live more than sixteen miles away, stand in the fourth corner." Ask each group to introduce themselves to others in their group and tell where they live.

Variations. You also can mix the groups after the initial pairings. For instance, you can ask people who live five miles away to form a new group with those who live more than sixteen miles away. Ask them questions that bring out the things they have in common, such as, "What are some of the things you like about our church?" Or ask questions that create understanding between divergent groups, such as, "Tell why you live where you do and some of the advantages and drawbacks."

Principles. This is a good way to find things you share in common with other congregants. This easily mixes young parents, seniors, and newcomers. Each question changes the makeup of the groups and helps people get to know each other.

United by Newness (Impact)

Submitted by Andrew King, lead pastor, Highland Village Church, Bloomington, Indiana.

Exercise Plan. Interview new members of your church with a video camera. This can be done in family units or individually with single adults. Utilize a set of common questions that are unobtrusive but deal with one of three FOR areas (Family, Occupation, Recreation), such as, "What can you tell us about your family [or occupation or recreation]?" The answers to these questions will tell you a lot about your new members. Then work with the interviewees to edit their responses into a two-minute video, introducing the family to the church. Play one or two of these videos each Sunday.

Variations. "After we completed this for new members," recalls pastor Andrew King, "we realized that the new members didn't know the older members. So we did the exact same thing for older members. Everyone enjoys it, and we continue this practice today." Due to time constraints, larger churches can do this within sub-congregational groupings of between 35 and 125 attendees.

Principles. Going out of our way to welcome newcomers and make them feel at home is a biblical admonition (Matt. 25:35–46; Rom. 12:13).

United in Creation (Impact)

Submitted by Joel Leichty, student, Wesley Seminary at Indiana Wesleyan University, Marion, Indiana.

Exercise Plan. During a worship service, church retreat setting, or similar environment where your attention is focused heavenward, ask participants to create an expression of their worship through art. Provide colored pencils, glue, clay, paint, decorative paper, fabric, or other materials, and invite participants to use whatever medium they like to contribute to a piece of art. Tell them this art should reflect the worship, celebration, and joy of all those present. Allow people to contribute either during a period of worship or quiet reflection. After the art is complete, ask people to answer the following questions: Why did you choose the artistic medium you did? What were you trying to communicate through the art you created?

Variations. You can do this almost anywhere. A youth group could create sand art while on an outing at the beach; a men's group could craft an outdoor altar out of wood for a worship service; and a women's group could create an elaborately laid out table of food for residents of a nursing home. In all of these activities, the uniting element comes from asking participants why they chose a particular medium, and what they intended to communicate through it.

Principles. Asking participants to explain why they chose certain artistic mediums as well as what they were trying to communicate tells everyone a lot about each other. The purpose of this exercise is not the art, but the deeper understanding the participants gain about one another's preferences and praises.

Carrying Out Communion (Impact)

Submitted by Adam Knight, lead pastor, University United Methodist Church (west campus), San Antonio, Texas.

Exercise Plan. Holy Communion is a means of grace that unites Christians together as sinners seeking God's forgiveness. On Communion Sunday, pastor Adam Knight's church cancels all Sunday school and Sunday morning Bible studies and encourages folks to all go to lunch together after the service. He tells people that part of feasting at the table of the Lord is letting that experience unite them as they live in the public eye. There is great camaraderie that comes from walking into the local Taco Cabana and seeing the love, sacrifice, and forgiveness that began during Communion continue to bind people together in public.

Variations. Adding table fellowship to church events lets people build on that unity over a meal. Jesus conducted some of his most intimate fellowship and teaching around the experience of a shared meal.

Principles. Seeing table fellowship as an outcome of Communion or another church event encourages congregations to live out their unity in visible witness to their communities.

THREE

THE CHURCH AS
A HARBOR OF SAFETY

EXERCISES FOR SAFE HAVENS

Violence . . . strides brazenly and
victoriously through the whole world.

—Aleksandr Solzhenitsyn

THE MIDDLE-EAST SPRING

The mobs surged across this Middle-East capital with a ferocity
and speed that caught innocent people in its wake. From his perch
high above the city, he could hear the cries of a city wrestling with
its own discontent. The sounds were heart-wrenching, for here
were a people in the pains of birthing a new future. But before
their new lives could emerge, they found themselves caught in a sea
of anguish, expectation, and violence.

He who stood on that hill knew the people's dreams as well
as their weaknesses. He had for many years surveyed their

quest, and now he was ready to lead them into a life beyond their expectation. But he also knew they were continually prone to violence that grew out of their peevish and self-centered nature. He had observed for millennia their spiteful inclination to segregate, exclude, and deride because of tradition, ethnicity, and gender.

On his perch overlooking throngs of dreamers and schemers, his heart felt heavy, as if it was breaking. His thoughts lapsed back to the image of a mother hen, who persistently and sternly gathers her chicks. And so too must he. He must sternly yet lovingly call them from this morass and mold them into a community of uncommon purpose. Overlooking such humanity in chaos and potential, he lamented: "Jerusalem, Jerusalem, killer of prophets, abuser of the messengers of God! How often I've longed to gather your children, gather your children like a hen, her brood safe under her wings—but you refused and turned away!" (Luke 13:34–35 MSG).

Soon Jesus would be lauded and celebrated amid these teeming throngs. And though Jerusalem had been notorious for killing the prophets sent to it (see 2 Kings 12:16; 2 Chron. 24:21; Jer. 26:20), they would one day greet Jesus with the words, "Blessed is he who comes in the name of God" (Luke 13:35 MSG).

But his mission would begin by wading into their chaos and meeting their physical and spiritual needs. To "the Fox," their Jewish-Roman overlord named Herod, the crowds looked like nothing more than a rabble mob.[1] But Jesus saw their potential as a people who could grow in their compassion, forgiveness, and transformation.

THE POWER OF THE CHURCH

Those Called Out

The word most used in the New Testament for church is the word *ekklesia*, a combination of two Greek words: *ek* (meaning "from" or "out of") and *kaleo* (meaning "to call"). The term was customarily used to describe people who were "called out for a civic duty."[2] But Jesus adapted this term to describe those who would follow him and be called out from a secular realm of violence and fear, into a new faith community of transformation, compassion, and forgiveness.

Jesus' use of this term would have startled yet inspired his hearers. Rarely was it used in connection with religious activities, and it carried the weight of a duty, an obligation, and even something that might not be pleasurable. Jesus' terminology hinted that he intended the church to be a people that would detach from the violence, segregation, and degradation to which they were accustomed. They would soon be filled with his Holy Spirit (John 16:5–15), and through this Spirit, they would become a compassionate kinship able to navigate their spiritual journey in the midst of a violent world. Jesus' statement, "I will build my church" (Matt. 16:18) reminded them that this would be *his* called-out community. It would be different from its civic counterparts. His would be a community that would model his reconciliation and restoration. And it would prevail in this purpose only as it stayed connected to him.

The Great Commandment

Let's dig deeper into how the church was to accomplish this. It may startle some to know that Jesus' Great Commandment is not the Great Commission to make disciples (Matt. 28:18–20).[3] The Great Commission is the church's goal, purpose, and aim.

But in the Great Commandment, Jesus addressed the human trait with which people struggle the most—to love and prefer ourselves above our neighbors and even God. So when Jesus issued his utmost command, this Great Commandment was, above all else, to "love the Lord [and] love your neighbor" (Matt. 22:37–39).

This is not to suggest that the Great Commission is any less binding or relevant. In fact, it is the purpose toward which the church is called.[4] Unless the church participates in God's mission to reconnect and reconcile with his wayward offspring, the greatest need of humanity has been deprived (see chapter 8 for more on this). But though the Great Commission is our aim, the Great Commandment is *how* we carry it out. Jesus stated it this way: "'Love the Lord your God with all your heart and with all your soul and with all your mind.' This is the first and greatest commandment. And the second is like it: 'Love your neighbor as yourself'" (Matt. 22:37–39).[5]

So Jesus called his church to come out from among the restless divisiveness of Jerusalem and be an avenue for God's remarkable love for neighbor and God. The words the biblical authors used for God's love in the Old Testament (*chesed*) and New Testament (*agape*) described God's steadfast, committed, and pursuant love.[6] This uncommonly potent and persistent love was the love the church was to reflect.

THE POWER OF A SAFE HAVEN

As Aleksandr Solzhenitsyn reminds us, "Violence . . . strides brazenly and victoriously through the whole world."[7] Even the casual reader knows that humanity's inhumanity is on the rise.

Solzhenitsyn continues, "The whole world . . . is being flooded with the crude conviction that force can do everything and right-eousness and innocence nothing."[8]

Into this cruel milieu of increasing brutality, God has planted his church. Not far from even the most violent and brutal streets in America probably stands a church building. God has salted his world with life-giving outposts of compassion, relief, and reconciliation. If only the church would remember and live anew Christ's Great Commandment.

This chapter will focus on exercises that can grow people and parishes into safe settings of physical and spiritual restoration. In a world where violence floods our senses, God has called a community to spread his uncommon love through his harbors of safety.

PRINCIPLES OF A SAFE HAVEN

Not Condemnation but Aid

Shunning and shaming is a tactic that rarely works when peo-ple are suffering. Chiding people with statements such as, "You are wrong. You are sinning!" is usually not productive. In fact, Jesus emphasized that conviction of sin is not the church's job when he said:

> If I don't go away, the Companion won't come to you. But if I go, I will send him to you. When he comes, *he will show the world* it was wrong about sin, righteousness, and judgment. *He will show the world* it was wrong about sin because they don't believe in me. *He will show the world* it was wrong about righteousness because I'm going to

the Father and you won't see me anymore. *He will show the world* it was wrong about judgment because this world's ruler stands condemned." (John 16:7–11 CEB, emphasis added)

Jesus' repeated use of "he will show the world" reminded his hearers that despite the tendency of religious people to condemn and shame, conviction was the duty of the Holy Spirit. The human role is to pray and rehabilitate, not persecute. The church's task is thus to provide aid with candor and honesty. Such a church becomes not so much an abode of recluse saints, as a community of caregivers.

Unfiltered Agape Love

To help those ravaged by violence and abuse, the church must be a font of unrelenting and unfiltered love by reflecting the *agape* (and *chesed*) love of the heavenly Father. Cambodian refugee Somaly Mam movingly writes, "I strongly believe that love is the answer and that it can mend even the deepest unseen wounds. Love can heal, love can console, love can strengthen, and yes, love can make change."[9]

> Love is the answer and that it can mend even the deepest unseen wounds. Love can heal, love can console, love can strengthen, and yes, love can make change.

Unfiltered love does not mean turning a blind eye or disregarding sin. Rather, unfiltered love is truthful love that is not filtered by contempt, disapproval, scorn, or oddity. Unfiltered love emerges when caregivers realize that but for the mercy of God they could be in the same predicament and in need of the same consolation.

Everyone in a safe haven church seeks his or her role in caregiving. Everyone seeks to do one's part in fostering an environment of love and health,

> Unfiltered love is truthful love that is not filtered by contempt, disapproval, scorn, or oddity.

where the ill-treated and injured can recover.

Take the Ill-Treated into Our Daily Lives and Homes

A helpful Scripture that sums up the importance of a safe haven is Romans 15:7. Paul, addressing the divided world illustrated in the story that began this chapter, stated, "So welcome each other, in the same way that Christ also welcomed you, for God's glory" (CEB). The word the Common English Bible translates "welcome" is translated in other versions as "accept" (for example, the NIV). The idea communicated by this Greek word "is to take something or someone to oneself, illustrated by inviting someone into your home."[10] Therefore, this Scripture might be paraphrased as: "In the same way that Christ also welcomed you, for God's glory, you the church should take the stranger into your life in all the ways that would mirror taking them into your personal residence."

This would include meeting their emotional needs and daily physical needs. Today, when so many people have suffered violence striding brazenly and victoriously through their world, it is critical that the church see its task as not an intermediary (pointing those in need to others), but as primary caregivers (meeting others' needs directly).

Compassion and Assistance for the Ill-Treated

As we create safe havens, taking more and more people into our faith communities, all Christians must grow in their abilities to render effective assistance. Our human inclination is to be self-seeking and to pull back from others' needs. Putting ourselves first and then meeting the needs of others becomes difficult.

However, to overcome this limitation, it is helpful to recall that humans are created in the image of God (Gen. 1:26–27). So Christians should reflect God's image in their actions. But how do we live out God's image? It becomes easier if we follow theologian Anthony Hoekema's suggestion that the image of God is best viewed as a verb rather than a noun. Hoekema states, "We should think of the image of God . . . not as a noun but as a verb: we no longer image God as we should; we are not being enabled by the Spirit to image God more and more adequately; some day we shall image God perfectly."[11] So the church's task is to image or model God more clearly through daily welcoming and attending to those ravaged by a heartless world.

Standing Up for Those Ill-Treated

Being created in the image of God also means that all people, regardless of how they feel about their heavenly Creator, are nonetheless created in his image. This requires the church to hold accountable any person who tramples that image, for such action offends God and should also offend the church. Oscar A. Romero stated: "As holy defender of God's rights and of his images, the church must cry out. It takes as spittle in its face, as lashes on its back, as the cross in its passion, all that human beings suffer, even though they be unbelievers. They suffer as God's images. . . . Whoever tortures a human being, whoever abuses a human being, whoever outrages a human being abuses God's image, and the church takes as its own that cross, that martyrdom."[12]

Safe-haven churches are thus not only settings for healing, but also for advocacy. They remain connected to the downtrodden and disheartened; standing up for their rights as well as giving them a pathway back to health. The following exercises are designed to assist churches in returning to that ministry.

EXERCISES TO CREATE SAFE HAVENS

I Must Cry Out (Intimacy)

Exercise Plan. Recall someone who was ill-treated. What happened? Who did the ill-treatment? Could someone say it was justified? What does it mean that all of humanity is created in God's image? (Consult these Scriptures if needed: Gen. 1:26–28; 5:1–3; 9:6; Rom. 8:29; 2 Cor. 3:18; Eph. 4:22–24; Col. 3:9–10.)

Reread the quote by Oscar Romero on the previous page. Then rewrite it in a way that is relevant to your situation. For example, "As holy defender of God's rights and of his images, *I* must cry out. *I must* . . ."

Variations. Do this as a group exercise. It is especially helpful for ministry groups that are reaching out to help others. This can help codify and focus the vision for their mission.

Principles. The church has a calling to stand up for God's principles in a loving, yet steadfast way. This helps congregants understand how and in what ways they can be the light of the world while doing so in a tactful manner.

Making Our Way on the Cruel Edges of the World (Intimacy)

Exercise Plan. Look at the Scriptures below that describe the mistreatment Jesus received:

- Isaiah 53:2–7
- Matthew 26:36–40
- Matthew 27:27–50
- Mark 10:33–34
- Mark 15:1–40
- Luke 9:58
- Philippians 2:7–8

Then read 1 Peter 2:21–23. What have you learned from these Scriptures? Write a paragraph describing how you might explain to a person in need Jesus' solidarity with the needy. Share this with two churchgoing friends and two non-churchgoing friends. Then rewrite your paragraph and keep it in your Bible next to 1 Peter 3:15.

Variations. Read Hebrews 11:32–37 from a modern translation. Then apply the same question above and write a paragraph describing how you might explain a person of faith's solidarity with the needy to someone in need.

Principles. This exercise reminds us that amid the security and luxury that many enjoy in the industrialized world, the Bible praises women and men of faith who undergo poverty, persecution, and torture for the sake of God's mission. This reminds us of the personal sacrifice that can be required to bring the good news to those in need.

Recall a Safe Haven (Impact)

Exercise Plan. Recall a time when you needed a safe haven, then answer the following questions: When was that time you needed a safe haven and why did you need it? What would the ideal safe haven you needed look like? How can your life or church become such a haven?

Variations. This is another exercise that can be utilized by a group, especially by a ministry planning team. In such environments, it is important not to be too revealing, but such environments can lead to more relevant and effective ministry.

Principles. By looking at your own personal times of need, you can better understand others in their need. And fostering an image of what kind of safe haven you needed can help you design safe havens that will help others.

The Danger of Neglecting Charity (Impact)

Exercise Plan. Most people recall Jesus' admonition that "whatever you did for one of the least of these brothers of mine, you have done for me" (Matt. 25:40). But few recall the context. Ask leadership teams to read the rest of Jesus' statement (Matt. 25:41–46) and then answer the questions that follow about their ministries: What was Jesus saying about the church, its neighbors, and its deeds? What do you think verse 46 means? That the righteous ones will go into eternal life? What does knowing this tell you about the importance of the church being a harbor of aid and safety? What will you do differently in the future to ensure you heed Jesus' admonition?

Variations. This exercise can also be undertaken personally, with revealing results. In addition it can be employed by new ministries being launched at a church. This exercise can be a helpful way for leaders to begin to focus on the needs of others and not just their own wishes.

Principles. Jesus' admonition reminds us of the eternal nature of addressing (or not addressing) the needs of "the least of these." While most Christians understand the importance of good deeds, few recall this passage and its warnings about their neglect.

The Shoes of the Suffering (Impact)

Submitted by Steve Wallace, associate pastor, River Church South, Gonzales, Louisiana.

Exercise Plan. The congregation—or those who attend a special meeting or session—breaks up into groups of no more than four to six participants. Facilitators provide each group with a different situation involving a hurting individual or family. A short paragraph-length story describes the difficult circumstance: loss of a job, terminal diagnosis, aftermath of an accident, challenge of an at-risk child, etc. Members of the group are invited to respond with wisdom, love, and the application of biblical principles, encouraging each one to better appreciate the challenging experiences at play in every congregation and the surrounding community. Afterward, groups share with everyone in attendance the insights they gained, inviting further discussion, understanding, and ideas for meeting the needs of people in need of a safe haven.

Variations. Every participant could be assigned one of the key roles within the challenging scenario, such as parent, child, neighbor, minister, teacher, coach, local entrepreneur, etc. The person would respond in character throughout the discussion. This is especially helpful when participants are acquainted with someone who needs a safe haven, but do not want to reveal their identity.

Principles. Even well-meaning and committed Christians tend to avoid difficulty, pain, and hurt. But most Christians also know that difficulties can help them understand the pain of others and how to best minister to it. There are so many situations for which congregants have little personal experience. To assume a role within such a story allows attendees to imagine what it might be like to walk a mile in the shoes of the suffering.

In his first epistle, the apostle John echoed the Savior, commending us to love others, activity that mirrors the love of God (1 John 3:17).

Fellowship Dinners (Impact)

Submitted by Joshua L. Henry, consultation coordinator, Church Doctor Ministries, Corunna, Indiana.

Exercise Plan: Most churches hold regular fellowship dinners designed to get congregants better acquainted. By changing the locale and recipients of these dinners, a church can learn about those in need. A church could move a regular dinner to the site of a homeless shelter or recovery center. To people in need of a safe haven, these dinners will take on a special and secure character. After dinner people can converse over coffee and dessert, providing a casual way for stories to be shared and spirituality discussed.

Variations. Your church may already offer a safe haven ministry, but it may be a ministry with which most of the congregation is unfamiliar. This exercise unites disparate ministries within a larger church. In addition some fellowship dinners should only be attended by specific segments of the congregation. For example, a dinner at a battered women's shelter might be best attended by mature women (in age and spirituality, see Titus 2:3–5) who could comfort and console the recipients.

Principles. It has been said that the church is a hospital for sinners. Christians can sometimes forget the excruciating urgency of those in need. A church can learn about the needs of others by fellowshipping more regularly with those in need. Such experiences can assist a church in providing a safe haven for the downtrodden, poor, and wounded physically, emotionally, and of course, spiritually.

FOUR

THE CHURCH AS A MOSAIC

EXERCISES FOR CULTURAL DIVERSITY

We don't want the ecumenical cooks to throw all the
cultural traditions on which they can lay their hands into one bowl
and stir them to a hash of indeterminate colour.

—John V. Taylor

HOPE SPRINGS ETERNAL

"We've tried different ways to become a multiethnic church,
and we've failed at each," summed up Rev. Steve Leon at the
end of an emotional town hall meeting at Hope Springs Church.
"I hope you can help us find the way, because we only have one
more effort in us." With some trepidation, I began putting
together a list of multiethnic options for this church. And despite
the optimistic name, Hope Springs Church was desperate.

The first thing I did was to visit Luis, the pastor of a nearby
Guatemalan congregation of the same denomination. The previous

year, he and Steve had tried to merge the congregations to no avail. The inability of Hope Springs' Caucasian congregation to merge with Iglesia Torre Fuerte's (Strong Tower Church) Hispanic congregation would launch my quest to map out for these churches the different ways that all churches can grow with cultural diversity.

Luis told a heart-wrenching story of how Iglesia Torre Fuerte had begun in his living room some six years earlier. When they outgrew the living area, Luis approached Steve about holding their services in Hope Springs' facility. The central location would make it easier for more Guatemalans to attend church.

"They welcomed us, but only so far," began Luis. "We were allowed to use the fellowship hall for our Sunday afternoon service, but when we got over a hundred people coming, I guess we started to bother them."

"How did you bother them?" I asked.

"I'm not sure. But we have a lot of young children, and I suppose they made quite a mess. And when we ran out of room and needed to move our worship service into the sanctuary, trouble really began."

Luis went on to tell of mounting arguments between the two churches over the use of the sanctuary. Steve later confirmed that Hope Springs' leaders were concerned that the general messiness left in the fellowship hall would spill over into the sanctuary. Finally, in what Steve thought was a flash of brilliance, one trustee suggested, "We can let them use the denomination camp on the other side of town. It's got an auditorium." The separation soon occurred, but the tensions increased.

"How did you feel about the camp?" I asked Luis.

"Like we were second-class," came Luis's reply. "It was cold in the winter, musty in the summer. It would be OK for a week-long camp, but not as a regular church home. I think they knew that."

"I didn't have a clue," came Steve's startled reply two weeks later. "We thought the camp worked better for them than sharing this building. But I guess we treated them like children. And we thought of ourselves as the parents. We even called them our 'daughter' church. There has to be a better way."

Today, Steve and Luis colead what I call a multiethnic alliance church. Iglesia Torre Fuerte has returned to share the building with Hope Springs Church. But both congregations have merged into one organizational entity. They truly function as equal partners now. The church has one administrative council, but representatives from both Spanish- and English-speaking congregations sit on it equally. And the best outcome is the level of reconciliation that is occurring between people of different traditions who are now equally sharing leadership duties in the same organization.

PRINCIPLES OF MULTICULTURAL CHURCHES

A Church of Many Colors (and Multiple Cultures)

Culture. Though the term *multiethnic church* is often used today, researchers prefer the term *multicultural*, because *culture* is a more accurate way to describe people who share similar behaviors, ideas, fashion,

> Culture refers to people who join together because of "learned patterns of behavior, ideas, and products characteristic of a society."

literature, and music. Christian anthropologist Paul Hiebert defined culture as people who join together because of "learned patterns of behavior, ideas, and products characteristic of a society."[1]

Behaviors are the way we act; ideas are the way we think; and products are the things we create such as fashion, literature, and music. Therefore, people of a culture can tell who is in their group and who is not by the way they talk, think, and act.

Ethnicity. Ethnicity is a type of culture, often based on biological connections to a geographic area of origin, such as Sri Lankans (from the Democratic Socialist Republic of Sri Lanka), Yemenis (from the Republic of Yemen), or Chinese (from the People's Republic of China). But the term *ethnicity* is very imprecise since there may be dozens of different ethnic groups that hail from the same area of origin. (Thus, the term *ethnicity* is not without controversy.[2]) For instance, China has more than fifty recognized ethnic cultures.[3] While all are Chinese, most do not think of themselves as primarily Chinese, but identify more with a culture based upon their traditions.[4] Therefore, because ethnicity is so imprecise, *culture* is the preferred term for describing people who link themselves together because of behaviors, ideas, and products.

Multicultural or Multiethnic Church? What should we call a church that reaches multiple groups of people? And what should we call a neighborhood that has Guatemalan Hispanics, Mexican Hispanics, aging Lutherans, and a growing base of young Anglo professionals? The accurate answer is a multicultural neighborhood. And such a mosaic of cultures should give rise to a multicultural church.

Below are examples of groups that have been identified as cultures:

- Affinity cultures (these are cultures that are based upon a shared fondness or affinity)
  - Motorcycle riders
  - Country music fans

- ○ NASCAR fans
- ○ Heavy metal music fans
- ○ Contemporary Christian music fans
- ○ Surfers
- ○ Urban scooterists (for example, UK mods)
- Ethnic cultures
  - ○ Latin-American
  - ○ Hispanic-American
  - ○ African-American
  - ○ Asian-American
  - ○ Native American
- Socioeconomic cultures[5]
  - ○ Upper socioeconomic level[6]
  - ○ Upper-middle socioeconomic level[7]
  - ○ Lower-middle socioeconomic level[8]
  - ○ Lower-working socioeconomic level[9]
  - ○ Lower socioeconomic level[10]
- Generational cultures[11]
  - ○ Builder[12] (or the silent[13] or greatest[14]) generation (born 1945 and before)
  - ○ Boomer generation (born 1946–1964)
  - ○ Leading-edge generation X (born 1965–1974)
  - ○ Postmodern generation X (born 1975–1983)
  - ○ Generation Y (born 1984–2002)

To help our churches grow in the most ways possible while recognizing the broadest variety of cultures, it is good to speak of multicultural churches and not limit our conversations to multi-ethnic ones. Multicultural churches are congregations where people from several cultures (ethnic, affinity, socioeconomic, generational, etc.) learn to work together.

Avoiding the Creator Complex

The Creator Complex. Sociologists have long known that people of a dominant culture will try, sometimes even subconsciously, to make over people from a subdominant culture into their own image.[15] One missiologist called this the creator complex and said, "Deep in the heart of man, even in missionaries, lurks that 'creator complex' by which he delights in making other people over in his own image."[16] When we encounter different customs, our creator complex wants us to view their customs as abnormal and change them to be more in keeping with our traditions.[17]

Sifting a Culture. The creator complex arises because it seems easier and faster to make a culture look like us than to try and sift out any impurities that run counter to the message of Christ. But in the words of missiologist Charles Kraft, every culture is "corrupt, but convertible."[18] To convert any culture requires sifting out elements that run counter to Christ's good news while retaining elements that affirm it. Eddie Gibbs labels this "sifting a culture," drawing from the image of a colander or strainer that sifts out impurities in food.[19] The fact that most purifying processes now happen in factories instead of in the kitchen may rob this metaphor of some familiarity, so a more contemporary term may be helpful.

A Cultural Filter. The term *spam filter* is broadly used to describe how computer networks separate unwelcome from welcome e-mails. A *cultural filter* may serve as a better image to depict a community of faith that is analyzing a culture, noting which elements run counter to the teachings of Christ, and openly filtering out perverse elements.

The Goal of Filtering: Spiritual and Cultural Reconciliation

What then is the goal for our cultural filtering? If, as Charles Kraft said, every culture is "corrupt, but convertible," then our purpose becomes to assist God in his quest to convert or transform a culture. Such transformation begins by reconnecting people to their loving heavenly Father. This has been called the ministry of reconciliation, which Paul described this way: "So we try to persuade people, since we know what it means to fear the Lord. . . . So then, if anyone is in Christ, that person is part of the new creation. The old things have gone away, and look, new things have arrived! All of these new things are from God, who reconciled us to himself through Christ and who gave us the ministry of reconciliation" (2 Cor. 5:11, 17–18 CEB).

In chapter 1, I mentioned John Perkins's suggestion that today's divided world needs churches that will foster physical reconciliation in addition to spiritual reconciliation. This would fulfill Jesus' prayer that his children be united as the Father and Son are united (John 17:20).

Today's youthful generations are more attuned to this need for reconciliation between people of different cultures. Today's young people have been born into a world divided by politics, economics, and cultural clashes. Yet across the nation I have observed churches led by young leaders that refuse to be limited by spiritual reconciliation. They also see maturity in Christ as advancing cultural reconciliation. I agree with Brenda Salter McNeil, who in addition to a spiritual reconciliation, sees "a host of people from various tribes, nations, and ethnicities who are kingdom people called to do the work of racial reconciliation."[20]

To bring about both spiritual and cultural reconciliation, we need churches where people of differing cultures are not only reconnecting with their heavenly Father, but also who are reconnecting with one another. A multicultural church may provide the best locale. Let's look at five types of multicultural churches to discover which type might be right for your church.

FIVE TYPES OF MULTICULTURAL (MOSAIC) CHURCHES

Multicultural congregations fall into roughly five types. In each category, I have codified examples from many authors, along with my own case study research to present a clearer picture of the multicultural options for today's church (along with the pros and cons of each approach).

The Multicultural Alliance Church

Figure 4.1

This church is an alliance of several culturally different sub-congregations. Daniel Sanchez describes it as one church "comprised of several congregations in which the autonomy of each congregation is preserved and the resources of the congregations are combined to present a strong evangelistic ministry."[21] The different cultures form an alliance as one organizational entity in which they equally:

- Share leadership duties (for example, leadership boards are integrated),
- Share assets (the church is only one nonprofit 501c3 organization),
- Offer separate worship expressions (to connect with more cultures), and
- Offer blended worship expressions (to create unity).

Offering multiple worship options allows the multicultural alliance church to reach out and connect with several different cultures simultaneously.[22] This makes it more evangelistically relevant and potentially effective. Plus, a regular blending of traditions in one service creates unity amid this diversity.[23]

A weekly format of a multicultural alliance church (with five sub-congregations) might look like this:

- Saturday, 6:00 p.m. Sub-congregation 1—Emerging worship service appealing to people in their twenties and thirties (usually without children).[24]
- Sunday, 9:00 a.m. Sub-congregation 2—Traditional worship service appealing to Anglo members of the congregation.
- Sunday, 10:30 a.m. Sub-congregation 3—Contemporary worship service appealing to Anglos in their forties and fifties, held in one auditorium of the facility.
- Sunday, 10:30 a.m. Sub-congregation 4—Asian-American worship service, held in another auditorium of the church facility.
- Sunday, 12:30 p.m. Sub-congregation 5—Hispanic worship service with a meal beforehand.
- Sunday, 6:00 p.m. Entire church—Unity service where all cultures are invited, celebrated and share rotating duties.[25]

Reconciliation occurs at a high degree in this structure because separate cultures work together as equal partners to run the church, while allowing each culture to celebrate their own

> Reconciliation across cultures is best fostered when separate cultures work together as equal partners to run the church.

traditions. Working together to run a church creates more unity than just sitting next to each other in worship. (As the Hebrew word for worship implies, it is God-directed, not neighbor-directed, reconciliation.[26])

The multicultural alliance church has three distinctive features:

- Several culturally diverse worship expressions (fostering evangelistic effectiveness better than a blended format because it concurrently connects with multiple cultures),
- Regular unity worship expressions (to create cross-cultural understanding and awareness), and
- One organization comprised of an alliance of sub-congregations (to foster collaboration, conciliation, resource sharing, and reconciliation).

Figure 4.2

STRENGTHS AND WEAKNESSES OF THE MULTICULTURAL ALLIANCE CHURCH	
Name	The Multicultural Alliance Church; also called Peer-to-Peer Congregations, Networked Church, Multi-Congregational Model, Multi-venue/site Church
Mode of Growth	Internal planting: starting new sub-congregations that are part (or internal) of the existing organization.
Relationships	Relationships are mostly equal, as cultures learn, lead, and share on an equal basis.
Pros	• Cultures work together leading a church. • Evangelism is greater because of multiple cultural entry points. • Assets and resources are shared. • If one culture is waning (an Anglo culture for instance), the emerging culture can more easily take the baton of leadership *continued*

Figure 4.2   *continued*

STRENGTHS AND WEAKNESSES OF THE MULTICULTURAL ALLIANCE CHURCH	
Cons	• Unity events must be regularly employed to offset any silo effect (separateness or polarization). • Conflict resolution skills are needed. • Leaders must foster multicultural teamwork. • Sunday morning services may still be a segregated hour.
Degree of Difficulty	High. It requires different cultures to work together in close proximity through multicultural committees.
Creator Complex	Low. Working closely creates cross-cultural understanding. In addition, waning cultures see themselves not only as handing the baton to the emerging cultures, but also as leaving a legacy.
Redistribution	High. Since all assets are shared equally, those of less-wealthy cultures have full access to the assets of wealthier cultures.
Relocation	High. Multiple locations can be under the umbrella of one central organization. Locations in wealthier areas can support locations in lower economic areas.
Reconciliation	Mid to high. Sharing leadership and assets forces cooperation, understanding, and reconciliation.

The Multicultural Partnership Church

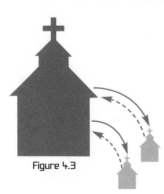

Figure 4.3

Here, a congregation, usually in a more affluent position, partners with a church in a financially struggling culture to help. This often occurs when a church in a growing suburb partners to help one or more struggling urban congregations. Al Tizon and Ron Sider in their helpful book *Linking Arms, Linking Lives*, share many success stories regarding how wealthier churches are redistributing their wealth through a financial partnership with urban congregations.[27]

Figure 4.4

STRENGTHS AND WEAKNESSES OF THE MULTICULTURAL PARTNERSHIP CHURCH	
Name	The Multicultural Partnership Church
Mode of Growth	Supports/helps struggling and economically challenged churches become more effective.
Relationships	Relationships are primarily from sponsor to stipendiary (beneficiary). Some arrows in the figure above are dashed and others dotted to represent that these are vague relationships of different degrees.
Pros	• Easy to undertake because the benefactor does not need to become too engaged in the recipient's organizational or congregational life. • Congregations can quickly support less-wealthy congregations.
Cons	• Low cross-cultural interaction. • Stipendiary (beneficiary) can feel they are just receiving cast-offs or the surplus from the wealthier church.
Degree of Difficulty	Moderate to low. It requires only moderate cross-cultural contact.
Creator Complex	High. Influence flows from the wealthier church to the needy one. And wealth may be seen as a sign of holiness or supernatural favor (rather than a confluence of societal factors).
Redistribution	Moderate. Wealth is being shared, but at the discretion of the wealthier church.
Relocation	Low. The sponsoring church isn't moving physically. It usually only moves its money or at best sends its people temporarily (for example, short-term mission trips and work teams).
Reconciliation	Low to moderate. Usually only a small group of volunteers or the leadership from the sponsoring church will interact with the less-affluent congregation. The potential for the creator complex to come into play may mean that reconciliation is further thwarted because the relationship seems like that of patron to peon.

The Multicultural Mother-Daughter Church

Figure 4.5

This may be the most popular model in North America. Here, a mother church launches (or plants) a daughter congregation that is intended to become self-sufficient. The daughter church is usually a different culture than the mother church. For example, an Anglo mother church might launch a Hispanic church, a hip-hop church, and an African-American church. These daughter congregations are labeled external church plants, because the intention is for them to eventually become independent or external to the mother church's organizational structure.[28] Though popular today, there are many downsides to this option that are typically ignored.

First, because a sponsoring or mother church perceives itself as the parent, the influence (arrows in the figure) usually flows primarily from the mother church down to the offspring, rather than

> Unfortunately, churches learn that when we have differences, it is best to separate.

the other way around. Many times a daughter church will feel it has been relegated to second-class status and has little influence upon the mother church.[29]

Second, once the offspring is independent (usually within one to five years) and a crisis erupts in the offspring, the mother church will often not feel the obligation to come to its aid. One daughter church planter told me, "They were so glad to see us start. [And they] told everyone about us. But we have huge money issues now since we bought this building, and they won't come to our aid. They told us we wanted to be on our own. And now we are!" Regrettably, many once-idealistic church planters have echoed to me the same feelings of abandonment because they lack official ties to the mother congregation. Granted, official ties to the mother church limit the freedom of the daughter congregation. But official ties may increase longevity and reconciliation.

Figure 4.6

STRENGTHS AND WEAKNESSES OF THE MULTICULTURAL MOTHER-DAUGHTER CHURCH	
Name	Multicultural Mother-Daughter Church; also called Planted Churches, Church Plants, Mother and Child Churches, Offspring Churches
Mode of Growth	External planting: launching autonomous churches that are intended to be attractive to other cultures.
Relationships	Relationships are stronger from mother to offspring. Offspring has little influence upon the mother. Mother churches have waning responsibility to help offspring.
Pros	• Easy to launch churches of different cultures because the offspring does not have to reconcile with the status quo culture in the mother church. • Increases the number of churches in a community. • Increases the number of churches that a denomination can count as part of the denomination.
Cons	• Daughter congregations may be less likely to survive than internal plants (the alliance model).[30] • Change proponents who keep a church innovative, often leave the mother church for the offspring.[31] • Churches learn the coping mechanism of separating when they have differences. • Low multicultural interaction after the offspring leaves. • Mentoring of planted leaders diminishes as plant becomes autonomous.
Degree of Difficulty	Moderate to high. Requires different cultures to work closely for an initial period of time, but not long-term. Difficulty is much lower for the mother church and much higher for the daughter church.
Creator Complex	High. The mother church feels self-satisfied because it has planted many churches. But in reality, it has distanced itself from the cultural differences that bring a mosaic of cultural richness to the mother. Also, offspring may initially feel euphoric by newfound independence, but eventually sense it has been cast aside and/or segregated. *continued*

Figure 4.6   *continued*

STRENGTHS AND WEAKNESSES OF THE MULTICULTURAL MOTHER-DAUGHTER CHURCH	
Redistribution	Moderate. Money primarily flows at the mother church's discretion from mother to child, with little cogenerated decisions on spending and asset utilization.
Relocation	Moderate. Only part of the congregation (the external daughter) relocates. The mother church creates segregation through a seemingly noble tactic of planting.
Reconciliation	Low to moderate. The relationship is based upon a benefactor (mother) allocating at her discretion to a beneficiary (daughter).

The Multicultural Blended Church

The blended church may be the second most common type of multicultural church. Most of its worship celebrations blend or mix several different cultural styles of music and liturgy. For

example, a seventeenth-century hymn may be followed by African music, followed by Hispanic or Asian songs, and sermon illustrations from Native American stories. The idea is to celebrate varied cultural traditions in one worship service.

Such worship in a blended format is laudable, and can create a degree of cross-cultural

Figure 4.7

sensitivity. But it may also be weaker in its outreach potential because it is less relevant to people who identify strongly with their cultural traditions.[32] People from subdominant cultures usually adapt to the dominant culture in one of three ways.

Consonant Adapters. These are people from an emerging culture who adapt almost entirely to the dominant culture. Over time they will mirror the dominant culture in behavior, ideas, and products. They will usually be drawn to a church that reflects the dominant culture.

Selective Adapters. These people adapt to some parts of a dominant culture, but reject other aspects. They want to preserve their cultural heritage, but will compromise in most areas to preserve harmony.[33] They can be drawn to the blended model because it still celebrates (to a degree) their culture.

Dissonant Adapters. These people fight to preserve their culture in the face of a dominant culture's influence.[34] Dissonant adapters may find the blended format of the multicultural blended church too inauthentic and disingenuous to their strongly held cultural traditions.

Not surprisingly, the multicultural blended church usually attracts those who are selective adapters. But two problems arise.

First, those who prefer blending will usually become a separate culture themselves. Blending over time creates a new culture of people who prefer blending. People who prefer to blend together several cultures are usually people who are more educated, wealthy, well-traveled, and integrated.[35] The blended church appeals not so much to multiple cultures, but to a culturally blended culture that emerges.

Second, blended churches are not as effective at reaching people who highly value and identify with their culture.[36] For example, if a person is a dissonant adapter and highly values his Guatemalan heritage, he may not attend a worship service where his heritage is just one sandwiched in among many. One associate pastor told me, "I'm proud that I am Guatemalan. I don't want to go to a church where Anglos lump all Hispanic people together in one service. I want to celebrate my Guatemalan culture." A church that offers only blended options often fails to connect with people who strongly identify with their cultural traditions.[37]

Still, such blended celebrations are needed at times. They are ideal venues for creating unity and conciliation as people grow in their appreciation for other cultural differences. They should be part of our strategies. However, the best place for them may be as blended unity services in a multicultural alliance church model.

Figure 4.8

STRENGTHS AND WEAKNESSES OF THE MULTICULTURAL BLENDED CHURCH	
Name	Multicultural Blended Churches; also called World-Beat Churches, International Churches, Intercultural Churches, Umbrella Churches
Mode of Growth	Blending cultures into a new intermingled culture. Appeals mostly to an upwardly mobile educated populace.
Relationships	Relationships are numerous but often duplicated; cultures less represented have less influence.
Pros	• Foretaste of what heaven will look like (Rev. 7:9). • Attractive to educated, middle/upper-class, and widely traveled people. • Creates multifaceted cultural celebrations.
Cons	• Attractive to mainly selective adapters, people with less cultural identification. • Blend may have too many unfamiliar cultural elements to communicate well to dissonant adapters, people with a high degree of cultural identification.
Degree of Difficulty	Moderate to low. Moderate because it requires cross-cultural compromise in blended ministry. Low because selective adapters are more likely to appreciate blended elements from different cultures.
Creator Complex	Moderate to high, because those who embrace a blended culture may view others who prefer their own culture as less mature.
Redistribution	Low. Redistribution takes place primarily amid the middle and upper-middle class blended community.
Relocation	Low. A facility accessible to many different cultures is required in order to attain the goal of blending people, usually located in the middle and upper-middle class areas.
Reconciliation	Moderate. Participants are reconciling to a degree through their creation of a new blended culture.

The Cultural Assimilation Church

Figure 4.9

This is actually not a multicultural church. This is a church where the dominant culture tries to make over other cultures in its image. One researcher described it as the dominant culture opening "their doors for the ethnics to come to *their* churches and worship God in *their* way with predictable lack of success."[38]

There are churches in North America today that embrace the assimilation model in hairstyles, clothing styles, music, etc. They believe that newcomers will mature faster in their faith if they adopt the congregation's preexisting traditions. These churches can give the impression that their culture is superior to other cultures (and they may actually believe it). Assimilationists may even insinuate that non-Anglos should be come whiter. But theologians cry foul, with one stating, "The New Testament precedents strongly asserted that the gospel was not intended to make Gentiles more Jewish, and Jewish more Gentile, but rather that each culture was to maintain its integrity in the body of Christ."[39]

Figure 4.10

STRENGTHS AND WEAKNESSES OF THE CULTURAL ASSIMILATION CHURCH	
Name	The Cultural Assimilation Church; also called Assimilationist Church, Colonialist Church
Mode of Growth	Making more people over in the traditional image of the congregation.
Relationships	High between people who have assimilated, but almost nonexistent between congregants and outside cultures.
Pros	• The church is united in culture; cultural differences do not need to be addressed. • The church only needs to have one type of worship style, language, etc. *continued*

Figure 4.10 *continued*

STRENGTHS AND WEAKNESSES OF THE CULTURAL ASSIMILATION CHURCH	
Cons	• The church creates an often old-fashioned culture which may become a barrier to contemporary nonchurchgoers. • Authoritarian leadership can arise, because forcing cultural adoption is seen as the preferred mode of discipleship. • Relationships with family, friends, and nonchurchgoers are damaged as a congregant assimilates to a new culture and disparages other cultures.
Degree of Difficulty	High. It requires willing participants to cast off their existing culture and accept a new culture in its place.
Creator Complex	High, because the church equates holy living with a specific culture. This domineering culture wants to make over other cultures in the image of itself.
Redistribution	Low, because people who refuse to assimilate are at worst chastised and at best ignored.
Relocation	Low, for the same reason as above.
Reconciliation	Low, for the same reason as above.

Creating Healthy Multicultural Hybrid Churches

In practice most churches are hybrids of the four principal multicultural types (ignoring the assimilation model for obvious reasons). For example, Times Square Church in New York City is well-known for its culturally diverse congregation. It uses a blended format for its Sunday worship services.[40] But Times Square Church also holds separate hip-hop worship services on Friday nights.[41] This is an example of the church behaving like an alliance model, because it is reaching out to two cultures at different times (blended culture on Sundays and hip-hop culture on Fridays). Though Times Square Church is famous for its blended Sunday services, it actually has grown because it offers culturally diverse celebrations at different times. Thus, a hybrid model of the above four types may also be the best choice for your church.

Use these models as discussion starters to see what kind of multicultural church the following exercises can help you become. As a result, your church can better participate in the personal and spiritual reconciliation a divided world so craves.

EXERCISES FOR CREATING MULTICULTURAL CHURCHES

Review Your Church's Multicultural History (Intimacy)

Exercise Plan. Look at the history of your church (as far back as you can go, up to forty years). Describe times when your church has been one of the following models:

- Multicultural alliance church
- Multicultural partnership church
- Multicultural mother-daughter church
- Multicultural blended church
- Cultural assimilation church

Based on this historical analysis and knowing what you know about your community, what will you do to help your church embrace a healthy model or hybrid of models for the future?

Variations. Apply this exercise to a ministry. Ministry programs are often organized similar to small churches.

Principles. Looking at how your organization or ministry has experienced multiculturalism in the past can help you avoid missteps in the future.

Review the Bible's Multicultural History (Intimacy)

Exercise Plan. Conduct a study on the church in the book of Acts and explain when and why it was one of the following types of churches:

- Multicultural alliance church
- Multicultural partnership church
- Multicultural mother-daughter church
- Multicultural blended church
- Cultural assimilation church

Variations. Other books of the Bible readily lend themselves to this exercise, including Luke, Romans, James, 2 Corinthians, and even Revelation. Church history is another good source upon which to apply this exercise, including the pre-Constantinian period, the Reformation, the rise of the Holiness Movement, the Pentecostal awakening, the 1970s Jesus Movement, and the rise of evangelical Christianity.

Principles. This biblical study imparts a sense of God's joy in cultural variety. At the same time, it reminds us that though elements in every culture are corrupt, God sees all cultures as convertible."[42]

Review Your Personal Multicultural History (Intimacy)

Exercise Plan. Write a paragraph about each of the following questions: What is your cultural background? How closely do you adhere to cultural traditions? Do you have personal traditions? How closely do you adhere to those personal traditions? Knowing this, what kind of church would be the ideal Christian fellowship for you?

Variations. Ask a friend who is part of a different culture to answer these same questions and share their answers (as appropriate) with you. Describe the ideal church that would meet both of your cultural preferences.

Principles. This exercise helps people see how their personal cultural preferences affect what they want in a church experience and community. This exercise reminds us that with today's blended society and families, a multicultural church not only creates intercultural understanding, but also brings together friends and families.

Spend Time in Their World (Impact)

Submitted by Jan Paron, academic dean, All Nations Leadership Institute, Alsip, Illinois; and Joshua L. Henry, consultation coordinator, Church Doctor Ministries, Corunna, Indiana.

Exercise Plan. This exercise asks people from different cultures to share an afternoon immersed in a new culture. Congregants sign up to spend a Sunday afternoon doing so. Church leaders then pair up congregants from different cultures, considering age, ethnicity, economics, interests, etc. On the Sunday morning preceding this exercise, the sermon might be about the importance of immersing oneself in a different culture in order to better understand it. During the Sunday afternoon exercise, a young couple might go home with an older couple, a staff member might spend the afternoon with a college student, an usher might spend the afternoon with a worship musician, or a Caucasian might spend the afternoon with a Hispanic member of the church.

Variations. You can pair people by affinity groups. The key is not for either culture to try to assimilate the other, but for each congregant to understand a different culture better. As with all cultural exercises, you must be careful to not offend or overlook when making pairs. Therefore, pairings should only be suggested, not required. Some people in the church will form their own pairings for the day.

Principles. The goal of this exercise is to see how God works among diverse cultures. You will also begin to see how your own cultural nuances can affect your opinion of others.

Celebrate Diversity (Impact)

Submitted by Joel Liechty, student, Wesley Seminary at Indiana Wesleyan University, Marion, Indiana.

Exercise Plan. Many churches have "celebrate recovery" programs, offering support groups to help people overcome life issues. But this celebrate diversity exercise is designed to help a church visualize the diversity in its civic neighbors. The celebrate diversity exercise involves hosting an event where diversity within the civic community is celebrated. This event may include tables with food from countries represented in the community along with music from these diverse cultures. And by allowing several speakers from diverse cultures to share something they have in common (such as relationship with Christ), this event can foster appreciation for the cultural mosaic of their community context.

Variations. If a church is large enough (or is a multicultural alliance church) it can host a celebrate diversity event among its own congregants. This is a good way to honor the efforts of congregational leaders to encourage diversity. It also allows newcomers to connect with culturally diverse ministries within the church. In addition, rather than simply reading Scripture in your native language (like you do each Sunday) have the verses read in multiple languages. Find people in your congregation who know different languages and ask them to read the passage in that language alongside the native language.

Principles. This exercise can help congregants glimpse a picture of the multitudes that one day will surround God's throne. This event thus becomes a microcosm of Revelation 7:9.

Culturally Diverse Hospitality (Impact)

Submitted by Joshua L. Henry, consultation coordinator, Church Doctor Ministries, Corunna, Indiana.

Exercise Plan. Go to the US Census Bureau website and determine the highest population of residents from another culture who reside within a five-minute drive of the church's facility. Create a team from your churchgoers whom you sense have the gift of hospitality. Ask them to do some research by asking people of the culture you identified regarding how a church like yours could be more sensitive to and help them. Also ask your team to study specific elements such as food, music, customs, taboos, etc. Then ask them to present their findings to the congregation.

Once the church has received the findings, ask congregants to pray for opportunities to use some of the ideas that have been shared to become more hospitable to the other culture. Tell them this cultural sensitivity is so congregants can become more acquainted with them as friends and neighbors. Have them pray, asking the Lord to provide opportunities for them to meet the needs of these people and to pray with them. Tell congregants this is not an opportunity for theological or cultural banter, but rather an open door for the graciousness of Christ and his love to be reflected in congregants' care and thoughtfulness.

Variations. Leadership teams, special event teams, etc. can also be utilized to conduct this research and integrate it into their ministry philosophies.

Principles. This learning experience is what anthropologists call ethnography, or the survey of a culture to learn about and understand it better. Such exercises have been described as "listening to the voice of a people."[43]

FIVE

THE CHURCH AS A HEART-TO-HEART GROUP

EXERCISES FOR TEAM BUILDING

A small group of determined people can change the course of history.

—Sonja Johnson

SMALL BEGINNINGS IN A SUNDAY SCHOOL

"You can tell we hate to leave," began Margaret. "It's just that this sanctuary is such a comfortable place."

"It wasn't always like this," interjected Mark. "Dark, dank, smelly. The sanctuary had the smell of death about it."

As I looked around, I marveled at how different the sanctuary of Armstrong Chapel Church looked today. Dark red padded pews, newly restored stained-glass windows, and polished woodwork. To this generation, most now in their seventies, the beauty and care of the sanctuary represented a desire to honor God. And while younger generations might disagree, who was I to say that God was not honored by their loving care of their house of worship?

"Come this way," beckoned Gerry. "Some still like to go out the back, but I prefer the side doors into the fellowship hall. It reminds me what God can do through a small Sunday school class." As I passed through the double doors, I was greeted by a large and bright atrium with a glass roof. Here were more than seven hundred people milling about; some lounging on comfortable sofas and others chatting cheerfully on lounge chairs scattered across the room. Still others laughed across tables while sipping coffee in the church's café.

"The two other services got out a bit earlier than us today," continued Gerry. "But that's OK. There's still plenty of time to fellowship. Get a cup of coffee, and I'll find my daughter and grandkids. I want you to meet them." And with that, Gerry disappeared into a crowd of laughter, merriment, and smiles.

"Amazing, isn't it?" came Margaret's voice from behind. "To think, we were a church barely alive. Just over fifteen of us in a Sunday school class and most of us serving on church committees too. Only about thirty total in church on Sundays."

"This is a testimony to your church," I began.

"Not quite," interrupted Margaret. "It was the bonds of that Sunday school class that led to this growth. We banded together and worked hard through the series of pastors the district sent us. We relied on each other in that Sunday school, and slowly the church began to grow. It's been eleven years, and now we have three sanctuaries, almost all full."

"But I still prefer our old sanctuary," added Gerry, returning with two grandkids in tow. "We kept the old sanctuary just the way it was. But I'm glad we offer other worship options too. They connect with a lot of different ages."

"How did you come up with your strategy: books, programs, or what other churches used?" I asked.

"Partly," came Margaret's reply. "Our growth plan really came out of the environment of our Sunday school. It was a weekly place for us leaders to fellowship, dream, pray, and plan. I can honestly say that our weekly Sunday school meetings were where we supported each other to grow this church. Well, it's almost time for Sunday school. I still need it!"

THE POWER OF HEART-TO-HEART GROUPS

More Than a Small Group: A Leadership Laboratory

The story above illustrates how a group can bond so remarkably and deeply that they can survive deadly attacks upon a church's heart. But not all small groups attain this inter-reliance and perseverance. I learned from members of that Sunday school class that their small group had bonded after many tough years where a succession of inexperienced pastors had almost killed the congregation.

"Our Sunday school was the place we worked out what to do next," remembered Margaret.

"And it was the place where we sought God, insight from his Word, and advice from one another," added Gerry.

In other words, this was not just a Sunday school class, but a place to mull over the week's challenges, seek biblical insights, and learn from one another. In many ways, this Sunday school was a leadership laboratory.

This was a remarkable type of small group, and one that more churches would benefit from utilizing. The exercises in the following pages were created to help you transform your existing Sunday schools, Bible study groups, home fellowship groups, prayer groups, and even committees into groups that foster spiritual maturity, steadfastness, and vision.

Such remarkable small groups customarily include fewer than twenty people,[1] meet on a semi-regular basis,[2] and have participants who:

- Recognize their group as a subgroup within a larger organization;
- Have an informal or formal structure, such as a regular meeting time, place, or schedule;
- Share a sense of inter-reliance and mutual dependence;
- Communicate more intimately than they would in a larger group;
- Dream, plan, and innovate in a supportive environment;
- Influence one another and stick together; and
- Feel that their most intimate needs can be met through the group's help.

What Is a Heart-to-Heart Group?

A heart-to-heart group is a good way to describe groups that meet some or most of the above seven criteria. Participants are sharing at a deep emotional and heart level. And this intimacy and inter-reliance makes them the ideal venue for spiritual questioning, maturity, and creativity.

Figure 5.1

DEFINITION OF A HEART-TO-HEART GROUP

A heart-to-heart group can be any small group of three to twenty participants, formally or informally meeting within the church fellowship network, where deepening inter-reliance, closeness, and spiritual maturity are emerging.

In actuality *any* small group of people that meets together on a semi-regular basis is a candidate for becoming a heart-to-heart group. To foster such transformation, the exercises in this chapter were created to cultivate heart-to-heart groups among home Bible groups, prayer groups, Sunday school classes, Bible studies, worship teams, sports teams, administrative committees, and more.[3]

Why Are Heart-to-Heart Groups Important?

As we saw in the story that began this chapter, heart-to-heart groups play an important role in helping people stay connected to a church and plan for its future even when the church is undergoing conflict, challenges, and discord. Figure 5.2 lays out some of the benefits of small groups.

Figure 5.2

BENEFITS OF HEART-TO-HEART GROUPS
It was in small intimate group settings that Jesus: • Answered his disciples questions about theology, history, and the future.[4] • Modeled healing and how to pray for those in need.[5] • Rebuked the disciples' willful attitudes and ideas.[6]
Researchers have found that in healthy churches: • 77 percent of church attendees say their small group participation is very important for them.[7] • 64 percent say new members are immediately taught about the importance of small groups.[8] • "A member is almost guaranteed to leave the church or become inactive in the church if he or she does not get involved in an ongoing small group."[9]
Secular researchers have found that in healthy organizations: • "The small group is the unit of transformation."[10] • "[Small groups] will remain the basic unit of both performance and change because of their proven capacity to accomplish what other units cannot."[11] • "A small group of thoughtful people could change the world. Indeed, it's the only thing that ever has."[12]

Because small groups are so effective in helping people support one another and develop closer relationships, they have been a recurring theme in church history. However, different writers have often used different names.

Figure 5.3

POPULAR NAMES HISTORICALLY GIVEN TO SMALL GROUPS	
Class Meetings	• Class meetings included six to twelve people who met regularly for discipleship and accountability.
Band Meetings	• Band meetings, comprised of four to six people, were more intimate subgroups of the class meeting.[13]
Cell Groups	• Like the cells in a human body they should split and divide.[14]
Life Cells	• They are where the spiritual and relational life of a church flourishes.[15]
Kinship Circles	• They foster a sense of family.[16]
Smaller Communities	• They are smaller than the entire congregational community.[17] • They create a sense of intimacy and belonging in a larger congregation.[18]
Growth Groups	• Spiritual and educational growth takes place rapidly and efficiently in small groups.[19]
Heart-to-Heart Groups	• Heart feelings are easier to share in the small group's intimate milieu.[20]

Kent Hunter's heart-to-heart label has significant appeal, especially in this book which deals with the heart attitudes of a church. This label will also be helpful in reminding us that these groups revolve around heartfelt trust, vulnerability, and intimacy. Figure 5.4 illustrates how heart-to-heart groups can be distinguished from larger groupings in the church.

Figure 5.4

WHERE HEART-TO-HEART GROUPS FIT INTO CHURCH STRUCTURE			
Name	**Usual Size**	**Rationale for Name**	**Other Names**
Congregation	Varies	Everyone who regularly attends a church[21]	• Membership circle[22] • Regular attendees
Face-to-Face Groups	20–175	A subgroup of church attendees, where: • People know one another by face, but not always by name. • There is a developing recognition that you are part of my extended circle.	• Cluster[23] • Sub-congregation[24] • Dunbar group[25] • Extended family[26]
Heart-to-Heart Groups	3–20	A group where members know each other's heart attitudes, inner feelings, and weaknesses with a developing interpersonal vulnerability and mutual dependence.	• Sunday schools • Prayer groups • Home Bible study groups • Regular Bible studies of all kinds • Regular breakfast, lunch, or dinner groups • Discipleship classes • Recovery groups • Some administrative committees[27] • Task groups including music teams, technical crews, hospitality groups, mercy ministries, outreach teams, custodial teams, and any kind of team that meets on a semi-regular basis

From Five Dysfunctions to Four Hearts

Few books have had as much impact upon healthy small groups as Patrick Lencioni's best seller, *The Five Dysfunctions of a Team*. Many businesspeople have been encouraged to read this by a boss or superior. Yet I have found Christian leaders sometimes reject it because of its focus on a business model. While there are many insights the church leader can glean from this book, any reticence to adopt it is understandable because Lencioni is writing primarily for a business audience. And his advice, while valid, seems a bit insensitive to the church context.[28]

Nevertheless, in Lencioni's model, a type of heart-to-heart group emerges, where each part builds upon the other, creating a healthy, inter-reliant and productive small group environment. Lencioni sees this happening through five elements: building trust, welcoming constructive conflict or discussions, making commitments between team members, embracing accountability, and scrupulously attending to results.[29]

You can see from these that Lencioni's principles are valid for the church. And the following four-heart model adapts these elements to increase their relevancy to the church context.[30]

THE FOUR-HEART MODEL FOR SMALL GROUPS

Heart Attitude 1: Trust and Candidness

Lencioni was right. Before any team can thrive, it must at its core be bound together by trust. Lencioni defines trust as "the confidence among team members that their peers' intentions are good, and that there is no reason to be protective or careful around the group."[31] In other words, this attitude means I trust that I can be vulnerable and open with the group regarding my fears, hopes, and failures.

Regrettably, such vulnerability and trust does not characterize all groups. But what if it did? What if most small groups could undertake exercises to transition into heart-to-heart groups? What if administrative boards, such as trustees who regularly meet and iron out difficult problems, could begin to develop this kind of trust?

You could revolutionize your church's network of small groups if you use the exercises in this book to transform them into heart-to-heart groups. And that is one goal of many of the exercises that follow. In the following pages, you will find exercises to help you renovate run-of-the-mill small groups into remarkably uncommon heart-to-heart groups where trust and vulnerability foster spiritual maturity.

Heart Attitude 2: Accountability to One Another and the Mission

Lencioni emphasizes that another important component is "the willingness of team members to call their peers on performance or behaviors that might hurt the team."[32] Many exercises in this book will focus on helping heart-to-heart groups develop accountability among the participants.

But Christians have another accountability that is even greater than team accountability. Christians are held accountable to God for their participation in the mission of God (the *missio Dei*) to participate in the loving heavenly Father's quest to reconnect with his wayward offspring.[33] This attitude stresses an accountability not only to one another, but also to increasing our accountability to God's mission to reconcile humanity to himself.[34]

Heart Attitude 3: Discussion with Conflict Resolution

While chitchat is unbridled in many small group settings, it has been my observation that conflict resolution is not. Lencioni bemoans that most people avoid conflict, and "the higher you go up the management chain, the more you find people spending inordinate amounts of time and energy trying to avoid the passionate debates that are essential to any great team."[35]

Lencioni has observed that healthy small groups encourage open, free discussion with give and take, disagreement without disparagement, and challenge with compromise.

Scripture, along with John Wesley, reminds us that such interpersonal conflict is part of life. Proverbs 27:17 observes, "You use steel to sharpen steel, and one friend sharpens another" (MSG). And John Wesley said about this passage that a nonchurchgoer can be sharpened by "the company or conversion of [a] friend."[36]

Scripture also reminds us that unresolved conflict among Christians is not healthy or God's intent. Paul wrote in Ephesians 4:2–3, "Conduct yourselves with all humility, gentleness, and patience. Accept each other with love, and make an effort to preserve the unity of the Spirit with the peace that ties you together" (CEB). And the psalmist portrayed unity with wonderful poetic imagery: "How wonderful, how beautiful, when brothers and sisters get along! It's like costly anointing oil flowing down head and beard, flowing down Aaron's beard, flowing down the collar of his priestly robes. It's like the dew on Mount Hermon flowing down the slopes of Zion. Yes, that's where God commands the blessing, ordains eternal life" (Ps. 133:1–3 MSG).

Amid such depictions and exhortations, unity in the church is still not common. Consequently, a church and its heart-to-heart groups must practice exercises to address conflict and create unity. It won't happen by itself. It requires exercise. The exercises in this chapter will strengthen your church's ability to openly discuss and resolve conflict.

Heart Attitude 4: Results

If heart-to-heart groups don't have clearly defined results or outcomes, then the group may drift aimlessly until it degenerates into self-seeking and cliquishness. Lencioni calls this the "ultimate dysfunction of a team."[37] The reader will be all too familiar with church groups that have deteriorated into self-serving rumor mills and self-preservation societies that are unwelcoming to outsiders. The key to heart-healthy small groups is to define the specific objectives of each group and then measure up to them until the group has attained those objectives.

> The reader will be all too familiar with church groups that have deteriorated into self-serving rumor mills and self-preservation societies that are cliquishly unwelcoming to outsiders.

In chapter 9, I will suggest a health regimen, where leaders of heart-to-heart groups will create objectives for the upcoming year and report on their progress. The final key to helping groups transition into heart-to-heart groups is to ensure that all groups create specific objectives and then check in (at least yearly) to see if they attained them.

The Positions of the Hearts Remind Us of Their Purpose

The first heart attitude, *trust* (represented by heart 1 in figure 5.5), is where reliance and vulnerability create an environment for growth. Heart 1 is also adjacent to the word *in*, indicating that trust grows from the inward ministry between group participants. This reminds us of the importance of a foundational trust in which there is "no reason to be protective or careful around the group."[38] This allows the group to next grow clockwise, toward an upward accountability to mission and to one another.

The second heart attitude, *accountability*, is at the top of the triangle and reaches up to God (as God reaches down to us). Every team is not only accountable to one another, but also accountable to God and his mission.

Heart 3, *discussion and conflict resolution*, sits in the right quadrant of the model, next to the label *out*. This reminds us that when discussion and conflict resolution are exercised in small groups, it can also grow outward to foster discussion and reconciliation with those outside of the group. The goal of this heart is to have an atmosphere of deepening respect, restitution, and reconciliation with those both in- and outside the group.

Figure 5.5

THE HEART-TO-HEART GROUP MODEL

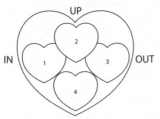

Heart 4, *results*, is what undergirds and sustains healthy heart-to-heart groups. Like the story that began this chapter where a Sunday school class took it upon itself the duty of keeping the church from closing, so too Katzenbach and Smith found that "a common set of demanding performance goals that a group considers important to achieve will lead, most of the time, to both performance and a team."[39]

EXERCISES TO CREATE HEART-TO-HEART GROUPS

Review Your Personal Small Group History (Intimacy)

Exercise Plan. Recall a small group that was unhealthy. Look back at the four hearts of a healthy team. Then answer the following questions: In which of the four hearts was the team deficient? How and why did this deficiency arise? What could have been done differently to overcome this deficiency?

Write a narrative (possibly including a timeline) describing how you would correct a similar team that was unhealthy and restore it to balance among the four hearts.

Variations. You can also apply this exercise to workplace teams, sport teams, prayer groups, Bible studies, and just about any small group of acquaintances that has become unhealthy.

Principles. By looking back and applying the four-heart model to a past dysfunctional group, the reader can see at what points (and for what reasons) the group digressed into a lack of health. Balance in trust and openness, accountability, conflict resolution, and productivity are critical for heart-to-heart groups to emerge within a church's infrastructure.

Fostering Trust and Candidness in a Small Group (Intimacy)

Exercise Plan. When have you been part of a small group in which you felt you had little or no reason to be protective or careful around the group? Do you have that kind of group today? What would you need to do to transform one of the groups in which you participate into that type of group? Give four steps to attaining this.

Variations. Apply this exercise to your family life, asking when you have been at a place that you felt you had no reason to be protective or careful around the group. You can also apply this question to your work environment to assist in attaining or regaining a candid environment. An alternative question for the above could be: When have you been part of a small group in which you felt you could be vulnerable and open regarding your fears, hopes, and failures?

Principles. Candidness and openness are necessary for small groups to become heart-to-heart groups.

Strengthening the Hearts of a Small Group (Impact)

Exercise Plan. As a small group, evaluate your group according to the four-heart model, by asking the following questions: Which of the heart attitudes are strong and which are weak in this group? Rank them in order from strongest to weakest. Which exercises from this book could help strengthen the weakest heart attitudes in your small group (transforming it into a heart-to-heart group)?

Variations. This exercise can be applied to any group of acquaintances that is ineffectual or unbalanced. You can also undertake this exercise with your group, using the results to collectively strengthen its heart health.

Principles. While some church groups today focus mainly on acquiring biblical knowledge or discharging some congregational task, any church group can enhance the spiritual growth of its participants by growing into a heart-to-heart group.

Team Reconciliation (Impact)

Submitted by Joel Liechty, student, Wesley Seminary at Indiana Wesleyan University, Marion, Indiana.

Exercise Plan. Assemble as a team and place in the middle of the group a bowl of warm water and a towel for each attendee. Read the biblical story of Jesus washing the disciples' feet (John 13:3–5). The humble act of a servant to wash others' feet can be a powerful visualization of reconciliation. Invite attendees to remove their shoes and socks. Quietly spend time in prayer, asking God to reveal to attendees any time when they offended or slighted other team members. As the Holy Spirit leads, allow participants to wash one another's feet.

Variations. Some denominations have regular services in which they conduct the ritual of foot washing, but the servant nature of this activity can sometimes be lost when conducted without preparation or too repetitively. Therefore, vary the locale and liturgy of the foot washing and reconciliation time. Though it should be conducted with some degree of privacy as humility and reconciliation demands, you can still include this as an element in retreats, Sunday school classes, or administrative meetings. Some small groups may want to conduct this as an annual ritual.

Principles. Jesus' act of foot washing made his disciples uncomfortable, but it also underscored the nature of a true servant. This was especially poignant to Peter, who at first protested such humility. This action serves as a living lesson of the humility Christ requires among those who follow him.

Two Sides of the Same Coin (Impact)

Submitted by Steve Wallace, associate pastor, River Church South, Gonzales, Louisiana.

Exercise Plan. Pair a team-building exercise with a service project. For example, a popular team-building exercise called Crossing the River requires team members to help one another cross a divide while carrying supplies and addressing multiple hardships. But what if you paired the lessons acquired in this exercise with a good deed, such as tackling the daunting task of clearing an overgrown lot, painting an elderly person's home, or pruning trees and bushes? Such service to someone in need will be heightened when coupled with the lessons just learned in the team-building exercise.

Variations. If either the service or the exercise is too time consuming, this exercise could be conducted on consecutive weekends. On the first weekend, church members visit a ropes course or outdoor activity center and complete a two- to three-hour team-building exercise. On the following weekend, they schedule a church work day that achieves two goals: the work is accomplished through shared responsibility and the team-building lessons are recalled before commencing the practical application.

Principles. Often institutions pursue team-building exercises because employees or other members of the group have found it difficult to get along and work together. A combined effort—linking team-building exercises and real-work projects—not only connects the lesson with the work, but ensures a more intentional, proactive approach to working together while not forgetting about the needs of others.

Where Do We Fit on the Third Wall? (Impact)

Exercise Plan. This exercise allows a group to see where and to what degree they are participating in God's mission. Give everyone in the group eighteen sheets of blank paper. Ask them to write what they perceive as the objectives of the group (up to six), with one objective per piece of paper. When everyone has listed their objectives, ask them to post their objectives to one wall, rearranging them into categories as they go. After everyone has posted their objectives, as a group further adjust the categories that have emerged. Post above each category the category name on a different colored paper.

Now do the same thing on another wall. But this time ask group members to write God's objectives of his mission. Provide participants with Scriptures that describe God's mission and our participation. Again, tell them to write up to six objectives, one per page, and post them to the other wall while placing them into categories. Post above each category the category name, again with a different colored paper.

On the third wall, the group leader will relist all of the categories from the second wall (God's missional objectives), then lead the group in discussing how their objectives from the first wall fit into God's mission. Based on the discussion, group members will post sheets of paper that describe how the group's objectives support God's mission. The goal is a ranking of the group's objectives based on the degree to which each supports God's mission. Then the leader will encourage participants to discuss ways that their group objectives can better support God's mission.

Variations. You can conduct this exercise with ministry leaders, such as the executive leadership team of a congregation. Or church oversight groups, such as church trustees or administrative committees, can conduct this exercise and then compare their results with the people doing the ministry. Seeing what oversight groups perceive as objectives versus what ministry participants see as objectives can help reconcile differences in expectations.

Principles. This exercise helps groups measure how vigorously and regularly they are supporting the *missio Dei*. And by comparing the results between oversight committees and ministry committees, you can adjust outcomes to fulfill everyone's expectations.

Taste of Small Groups (Impact)

Submitted by Gary L. McIntosh, professor of Christian ministry and leadership, Talbot School of Theology, Biola University, La Mirada, California.

Exercise Plan. This exercise introduces people to what small groups are like. At a regular church event, such as a unity Sunday or a church meal, the sermon or teaching is replaced by this exercise. A church leader prepares a brief talk about the importance of small groups, explaining how they fit into the church's personality and vision. At tables a different small group leader is assigned to prepare to lead a twenty-minute small group experience. He or she will place a sign in the center of the table to identify the type of small group meeting at that table (Bible study, interest group, prayer group, service group, sports group, etc.). Attendees are encouraged to "taste" the life of a small group by choosing a table group in which they may have interest. The event concludes with a presentation of upcoming small group opportunities and follow-up steps for those who are interested.

Variations. You can also invite people to a "surprise" event. Following the morning service, have people gather in a room for lunch. As people enter the room, tell them to sit at any table. Each table should have one small-group leader. Following a light lunch, the pastor steps forward to explain the importance of small-group ministry to the church. After a short talk, the pastor should conclude by saying something like, "Now let's experience a taste of small groups." At that point, the leaders at each table take over and lead the people in a small-group experience for fifteen minutes. Remember to tell your small-group leaders to not be pushy or overly intimate. Just let the camaraderie and fellowship of the experience unfold.

Principles. People like to test an idea before they commit to participation. And when people enjoy themselves, they are likely to want to continue in something that has brought them enjoyment.

SIX

THE CHURCH AS A WORSHIPING COMMUNITY

EXERCISES FOR ENCOUNTERING GOD

Without worship, we go about miserable.

—A. W. Tozer

LOST IN TRANSLATION

"It seems it's all about the sermon," began Phil. "And they don't even know they do it." My meeting with the church trustees that night had just taken a tension-filled turn for the worse. "The sermon seems to be the thing we spend so much time preparing and advertising for with video clips and charts and everything else. Everyone on the planning team seems to be all about the sermon."

This once-sizable congregation had been a worship innovator some fifteen years earlier. But now it was declining. And some on the board felt that Brad, a gifted pastor and orator, had unintentionally shifted the emphasis away from worship and toward the sermon. "We're an old historic denomination," answered Brad defensively. "And it's always been known for powerful preaching. I think I'm good at that. So when you hired me, I thought you wanted more of an emphasis on preaching."

"It's not that we don't appreciate the preaching, Brad," said Ron. "It's just that so much of our weekend effort goes into the sermon. And the thing we used to be known for, a place to encounter God, has gotten lost in the shuffle."

"Maybe it's easier," added Celicia, who was not known to interrupt often. All eyes turned to the young, twentysomething girl in corner of the room. "It seems like we need both. It's just that encounter with God is so elusive. Sometimes it happens; sometimes not. But I need it each Sunday. Maybe because worship is so hard to experience, we need to spend more time praying for it, preparing for it . . . seeking it."

THE POWER OF WORSHIP

Most Christians describe their Sunday morning gatherings as worship services, but really our gatherings are more than just worship. Teaching from God's Word is a big part of our assemblies. And enjoying one another's fellowship is an important element as well. So why then do we call these *worship* services?

A definitive answer might be hard to ascertain. But a plausible explanation is that in worship the natural and supernatural intersect in such a marvelous way that the connection between the two has emerged as a defining characteristic of our gatherings. Let's look at the words the Bible uses for worship to better understand this significance.

Defining Worship: Not Just Praise . . . but Come, Adore, and Wait

Not Just Praise. The English word *worship* comes from the Anglo-Saxon *weorthscipe*, a combination of the words for *worth* and *to ascribe*.[1] Thus, the word *worship* means "to attribute worth to something." We use it this way when we say someone worships money or worships one's career. Worship of God certainly entails praising him for worth and goodness. But the biblical authors had much more in mind and chose words that meant more than this.[2]

Come, Adore, and Wait. The most common Old Testament word for worship is derived from *shada*, meaning "to bow, to prostrate oneself."[3] And the most common New Testament word is *proskuneo* meaning "to prostrate onself, to adore."[4] Both of these terms are derived from the ritual of encountering a king or monarch.[5] The person would bow down in front of the potentate, often lying facedown in submission and adoration, awaiting the monarch's reply. This action demonstrated the subject's respect, contrite nature, and openness to admonition. The monarch would then instruct the subject.

Such an expression of submission and expectation is often missing in our churches, where festivity can take precedence. As a result, many worshipers are never given the opportunity to draw near to God and await his response. But the Bible reminds us that worship is a time for divine interaction and guidance.[6] We see this exemplified when, in the midst of worship, God counseled the Antioch church to "appoint Barnabas and Saul to the work [he] called them to undertake" (Acts 13:2 CEB);[7] and answered Paul and Silas's imprisonment with seismic liberation (Acts 16:16–40).

Defining Worship: It Takes Work . . . Inwardly and Outwardly

Working at It Outwardly. In the Old Testament, there is a second word that is often used in place of *shada*. It is *abodah*, meaning "to labor" and is often translated "the service of God."[8] This term reminded the hearers that genuine worship requires effort and preparation. Even the word we use today to describe the order of our worship, *liturgy*, comes from combining the Latin *laos*, meaning people, with *ergon*, meaning work.[9] Though worship is the intersection of the natural with the supernatural, those who have been involved in leading worship would no doubt readily agree with both Bible and history that encounter also requires preparation.[10]

Working at It Inwardly. Worship isn't just outward preparation. The labor of worship also means an inner labor to ensure that you are humble, contrite, and remorseful for wrongs and ready to draw close to your King.[11] Jesus underscored this when he reminded his hearers, "It's who you are and the way you live that count before God. Your worship must engage your spirit in the pursuit of truth. That's the kind of people the Father is out looking for: those who are simply and honestly *themselves* before him in their worship. God is sheer being itself—Spirit. Those who worship him must do it out of their very being, their spirits, their true selves, in adoration" (John 4:23–24 MSG; see also Luke 10:25–37).

A Missional Definition of Worship

Earlier in this book, it was noted that God's mission is to reestablish a relationship with his wayward offspring.[12] It was also noted that churches that participate in this mission have been called *missional* congregations. Therefore, knowing the history of the words for worship and knowing God's mission, we can more accurately define worship.

Figure 6.1

A MISSIONAL DEFINITION OF WORSHIP[13]

Worship is an intimate, supernatural, and ongoing reunion with the heavenly Father who created us, which requires on the part of his offspring humility, adoration, and effort.

The Missing Power in Our Churches

I have encountered too many churches where worship has become a hackneyed, unengaging jumble of styles, goals, and musicians with the purpose of creating celebration, not encounter. The words for worship in both the Old and New Testaments describe it as a supernatural encounter that requires humility, adulation, and work. Ralph Martin says that encountering God's holiness can be both *awe*-inspiring and fear-*ful*. Labeling this as God's "awe-ful" holiness, Martin writes, "The awe-ful holiness of God is a thread of teaching which runs through the entire Bible. In that awe-inspiring presence his servants are conscious of their finitude and frailty."[14] Rudolph Otto describes an encounter with such an awe-ful God as both attracting as well as frightening.[15]

> I have encountered too many churches where worship has become a hackneyed, unengaging jumble of styles, goals, and musicians with the purpose of creating celebration, not encounter.

In God's grace, he reaches out to commune with us in our frailty and fear. And even though God is awe-ful in holiness, "his love is so outstretched to us that we may come with confidence and with an answering love . . . (Eph. 2:18; Rom. 5:2; 1 Pet. 3:18; Heb. 7:25; 10:19–22)."[16]

The exercises in the following pages are designed to help your congregation approach this loving, seeking, and awe-ful God. And these exercises can help your congregation re-embrace the biblical heart of worship as an intimate, majestic, supernatural—and frequent—encounter.

PRINCIPLES OF WORSHIP

Conversations with God amid Hymns and Spiritual Songs[17]

In the Old Testament, we see that approaching an awe-ful God is arbitrated by songs of adoration, humility, and expectation in varieties of style, including antiphonal singing (Ex. 15:21; Num. 10:35; 1 Sam. 18:7), songs written for congregational singing (Pss. 24, 118, 134, 145), and even responsive singing between two choirs of musicians (Ezra 3:11; Neh. 12:24, 31). The New Testament gives further evidence of variety in song and vocal praise, as Jesus demonstrated when he sang the *hallel* psalm of the Passover meal (Matt. 26:30). And Luke recorded four hymns in his description of the birth of Christ: the *Magnificat* (Luke 1:46–55), the *Benedictus* (Luke 1:68–79), *the Gloria in Excelsis* (Luke 1:14), and the *Nunc Dimittis* (Luke 1:29–32). It is not surprising that James would recommend "Is any merry? Let him sing psalms" (James 5:13 KJV).[18]

Conversations with God for Help and Direction

In Acts 13:1–3, it was in the midst of worship that God directed the Antioch church to "appoint Barnabas and Saul to the work [he] called them to undertake" (v. 2).[19] And when cast into the Philippian jail, Paul and Silas sang and prayed for their miraculous release (Acts 16:16–40). As the Hebrew and Greek words for worship remind us, this is an audience with a gracious, heavenly monarch that wants to help and direct his offspring. Worship is not just about adoration, but it is also significantly about communication.

> If one purpose of worship is divine help and direction, then more time should be allotted and structure should be altered if this enhances our heavenward communication.

Too often today churches rush through worship because of time or structure constraints. But if one purpose of worship is divine help and direction, then more time should be allotted and structure should be altered if this enhances heavenward communication.

Conversations with God for Correction

Meeting a monarch and laying ourselves open at his feet invites not only his direction, but also his correction. He sees the sin in our lives, our wrong attitudes, and the wrong directions we crave to go. In the intimacy of worship, God can communicate with us his corrections to our courses.

An area that often needs to be addressed is our tendency to worship God while worshiping so many other things. God will not be lumped together with other objects of worship (Rev. 4:10–11, 13). One writer summarized, "There is an exclusiveness about loyalty to Christ which must be honored at all costs (1 Cor. 10:21)."[20] It is in the intimacy of worship that God often reminds us that we have put many other things ahead of him and that we must humbly return to worship him above all else (1 Tim. 1:17).

Conversations with God for Encouragement

There is nothing quite so encouraging as having an audience with someone who has the power to unselfishly help you. Worship is an encounter with a God whose unlimited assistance gives us confidence that we can accomplish almost anything if God is in it. C. S. Lewis, known for scholarly prowess, delighted in such worship encounters stating, "The most valuable thing the Psalms do for me is to express the same delight in God which made David dance."[21]

Conversations with God Should Be in One's Heart Language

God sent his Son to earth to speak our language and wear our clothes so that we could better understand his message. His coming was *in* the *flesh*, which is called the *incarnation* from the Latin: *in-* (into) + *carn-* (flesh) + *ation* (to become, to transform).[22] The word *incarnation* reminds us that God transformed himself to communicate face-to-face with us and in our vernacular.

The same should hold true for worship. God still seeks to communicate personally and in each person's language. In chapter 3, we saw that different cultures worship in different ways with different artistic styles, music, and rhythms. Researchers know that people worship best in artistic and cultural styles with which they are familiar.[23]

Kent Hunter calls the cultural language in which a person best communicates a person's heart language.[24] Hunter further describes this as "the language you dream in."[25] By this, Hunter means that when people dream, they often have a language in which they envision themselves speaking during that dream. This, according to Hunter, is their most natural language for communication. If worship is conducted in a person's heart language, then that person will be less distracted by unfamiliar expressions and aesthetics.

Since God is the master of all cultures, conversing unhindered with every one of them,[26] and since humans typically have one heart language in which they best learn and dream,[27] then it

> The cultural language and expressions in which a person best communicates is a person's heart language.

seems logical that God would alter his language without altering his message in order to better communicate with us. Worship leaders have a parallel task of fostering relevant worship in the heart language of the majority of the participants.[28]

However, too often worship leaders see their task as acquainting other cultures with new musical genres or styles (or with his or her own preferences). But worship is not primarily a place to teach others or even to reconcile cultures with one another.[29] Worship is biblically and primarily the place for humans to encounter God and seek his conversation. Reconciliation and direction flow out of worship; so the primary purpose of worship is for us to communicate with God, not communicate with each other.

EXERCISES TO CREATE WORSHIP

Recall a Personal Worship Encounter (Intimacy)

Exercise Plan. Recall a time when you experienced a supernatural encounter with God. How did you feel beforehand? How did you feel afterward? What did you experience in direction, correction, and encouragement? What can you do in the future to foster more times of genuine spiritual encounter?

Variations. Apply this exercise to the most recent time you were in a worship service.

Principles. This exercise allows a retrospective look at what occurred when you encountered God. This exercise also helps you see how God gave you direction, correction, or encouragement amid that encounter.

Recall a Worship Disconnect (Intimacy)

Exercise Plan. Recall a time when you experienced a worship disconnect. For example, this could be a time when you tried to connect with God to no avail. When was it? What happened?

Pick (or adapt) two or three of the exercises in this chapter and describe how you might use these exercises in the future to help avoid a similar worship disaster.

Variations. Apply this exercise to the most recent time you were in a worship service. What elements were disappointing? Now that you have read this chapter, what are three things you could do in the future to help prevent a similar worship disconnect?

Principles. Spending too much time analyzing missteps can create obsession with blunders and not enough time dwelling on God's blessings. Don't spend too long on this exercise. However, judiciously evaluating missteps in worship will help you see at what points (and for what reasons) a worship encounter began heading in the wrong direction. This exercise can form the basis for crafting alternative plans to avoid missteps in future worship experiences.

Praise E-Wall (Impact)

Exercise Plan. Create a website (sometimes called an e-wall) on the Internet where congregants can post their comments about when and how they felt close to God. (This could be a new webpage on your church's current website.) Invite insights with a question such as, "When did you feel especially close to God during a recent worship service? Tell how the Holy Spirit was moving and what you experienced."

Variations. On the e-wall, you can allow congregants to comment on other church events as well, but have them only identify the event and date. You can allow congregants to comment anonymously or by name. However, limit responses to only those from attendees. (To control this, use a hidden URL that is given out in church, perhaps in the bulletin, but is not linked from the church website or searchable from the Internet). This exercise can also be undertaken in a blog format. The same care in screening posts must be taken. A final variation is to use this exercise to poll the feelings of the church volunteers or staff on a regular basis.

Principles. This exercise's purpose is to allow constructive and helpful congregational feedback to help staff evaluate when and how spiritual encounter has occurred. This should not be regarded as a hard-and-fast assessment, but rather an opportunity to get a general idea of how the Holy Spirit is moving. Cynics and disparagers will usually give their feedback as well, but even if their comments are taken with a grain of salt, you can begin to see an emerging picture of how the Holy Spirit works amid your worship community.

Learn to Improvise in Worship (Impact)

Exercise Plan. Draw together all of the liturgical elements for a worship service. But during the actual worship service, let the Holy Spirit guide the leaders to put together the elements in a certain way. For instance, the worship team might prepare and practice three to five worship songs for the service. The preacher would prepare a sermon. Another person could prepare Old Testament and New Testament Scriptures relevant to the sermon. An artist might prepare a related song, poem, testimony, or artistic expression. The first step to successful improvisational worship is that the specific elements are prepared beforehand through prayer and preparation, but the exact order is not decided on before the service.

When the leaders and congregation join together for the service, everyone waits upon the Holy Spirit to arrange the order. One church did this by starting the service by quietly waiting for several minutes until the bass guitarist in the praise band began the first song. After that song, another pause of quiet reflection took place until the keyboardist sensed the Holy Spirit's leading to start a second song. Then a young lady with an Old Testament Scripture came forward and shared. This was followed by a leader who led the congregation in prayer. Next the pastor said, "I sense it is time for the sermon." After the sermon, other elements prepared beforehand were unfolded. What struck observers was how the leaders let the Holy Spirit create the order, rather than forcing worship to emerge from their preconceived configuration. The improvisational structure also made everyone, but especially the worship leaders, more sensitive to the moving of the Holy Spirit.

Variations. Churches that have historical liturgical patterns may find improvisation too uncommon for their congregants to accept. In this situation, churches can practice mini-improvisations by having the worship leader announce, "We have several songs picked out and a couple of Scriptures. We are going to spend a few moments in silent reflection and allow the Holy Spirit to lead us into how this next portion of our worship service will unfold."

Principles. Worship improvisation has been practiced for years by the Quakers.[30] Such waiting upon the leading of the Holy Spirit helps keep the focus upon the Lord's leading and not prefabricated liturgical structures (though as noted above, the elements of improvisation are still prepared beforehand). This can help create an expectation for encounter. Worship services can become mundane and repetitive compositions with the same layout week to week. Improvisational worship is just a new name for what churches have historically called "allowing the Holy Spirit to move."[31]

Liberating and Loosing the Laity (Impact)

Submitted by Adam Knight, lead pastor, University United Methodist Church (west campus), San Antonio, Texas.

Exercise Plan. Gradually allow lay leaders with emerging leadership skills to be in charge of more of the worship service.[32] This may also require you to limit the paid staff's participation. Try setting up a weekly or monthly rotating team of volunteers to oversee many of the worship responsibilities. For example, the first week of the month one lay leader does the welcome; the second week he or she prays for the offering; and so on. Then a preaching or teaching pastor is only responsible to preach in the service. When more laypeople are involved, you can observe God's heart for bestowing special gifts on them as well. This variety coupled with a nonprofessional point of view can make worship more down to earth, participatory, and engaging.

Variations. Allow emerging leaders to preach the sermon or conduct (as appropriate within your theology) the sacraments. You can also apply this exercise to other ministry duties including teaching courses and visiting those in the hospital.

Principles. This exercise helps ensure that worship is not a pastor or band show by involving as many laypeople as possible. Getting laity involved in all appropriate areas of worship helps engage the entire body of Christ in worship leadership and brings the people in to participate rather than become a spectator.

Worship Leader Exchange (Impact)

Exercise Plan. Invite the worship leaders from a church with a different style and culture of worship to come and lead worship at your church. If the other church is amenable, have your worship leaders reciprocate the favor and lead worship at their church. Remind everyone (including the worship teams) that this is an opportunity to worship God with aesthetics, rhythms, and styles that may be personally uncomfortable for them but are relevant to others. The purpose is to help people broaden their experiences through an encounter with the Holy Spirit via a different worship expression. This exercise helps people observe the Holy Spirit moving in dissimilar cultures.

Variations. Add testimonies from the worship leaders, so the congregants can hear firsthand how the styles that make them uncomfortable are relevant to someone else. Another variation is to conduct a teacher exchange to help a Sunday school class or small group see how God moves in different cultures.

Principles. This allows participants to grow in respect and appreciation for different styles of expression and art. It would not be wise to force this upon dissimilar cultures on a regular basis. This is because, as we saw in this chapter, trying to force people to worship only in a new way and not allowing them to worship in their heart language will get them frustrated by an inability to feel comfortable and connect with God. Rather, use this exercise on a semi-regular basis to breed familiarity, respect, and acceptance of different worship cultures. Remember, if you want to connect people to God, then you should encourage them to worship God in their heart language while respecting that others may do so in a different heart language.

SEVEN

THE CHURCH IN MISSION

EXERCISES FOR ENGAGEMENT

By leaving the ghetto behind, the church has implied that
its mission is meaningless to the poor, the hopeless, and the wretched—
except when an ocean separates the church from the ghetto.

—David L. McKenna

FAIR REWARDS

The office was very different from the pastor's office we had
just left. The walls were strewn with awards, and the center of
the room was dominated by a large mahogany desk. As the
mayor walked in, I could tell by his expression that it wouldn't
be good news.

"Look," he began. "The church sits right in the middle of the
city's expansion project. Now I know you've tried to get signatures
from community residents to support your cause. And I wish you
could stay, but without enough community support, my hands are

tied. Eminent domain gives me the right to take your church and pay you a fair price."[1]

"But we've been here for almost eighty years," interjected Leon.

The graying pastor of an equally graying church, Leon had nevertheless taken this bold step of meeting with the mayor in hopes of preventing the city from razing their church facility.

"Look, we're giving you a fair price," the mayor added in an increasingly irritated tone.

"It may be what the church is worth," replied Leon, "but it is not enough to purchase another building. We're an old church, and we've got old people. We just want to continue doing the good work we've been doing."

And with that Leon launched in on one of his lectures on his church's history.

"We are a missions church," began Leon. "Since the 1950s, we've been known around the country for our support of missionaries. We give over 50 percent of our income to missionaries and have for decades. If we die, so does that support that goes to many, many missionaries. We can't let that happen."

From there Leon continued uninterrupted for another five minutes until the meeting ended with little communication and even less compromise.

"I wonder what will happen to them," said Leon, as we walked back to the church building.

"It might be tough at first, but the missionaries will find other support," I answered.

"I'm sure they will," added Leon, "but I'm not talking about the missionaries. I'm talking about them." Leon was gazing around at the neighborhood we were passing: boarded-up buildings and homes in disheveled repair. Leon was glimpsing another mission field, just as in need as any mission field across an ocean. "These people were once part of our church. Maybe not them, but their grandparents. But we forgot about them. We got so wrapped up in people halfway around the world that we forgot about the ones in our backyard. We gave away, but we never grew. We sent, but no one stayed home to minister here. And now we're reaping our reward."

THE POWER OF THE CONGLOCAL CHURCH

A Term Is Needed That Emphasizes Balance in a Church's Outward and Inward Focus

There are many labels that are used to describe churches, and each seems to define a different style of ministry or history. But what if there was a term that could be applied to almost any church? And what if this term helped to remind each church that its focus must not be just inward toward its congregants, but also outward toward non-churchgoing people?

Some have tried to use the term *missional church* as a label for a congregation that is primarily outward focused. But this is an error. Remember, *missional* describes a church that is participating in God's mission to reconnect with his wayward offspring.[2] "Going out" is just one tactic to accomplish this mission. But *missional* means much more than just going out; it also means that a church is participating in ministry inward to the congregants, helping them mature in their knowledge of their loving heavenly Father and assisting them as they discover the spiritual gifts he has given them.

Therefore, a church that effectively participates in God's mission has a dual thrust. Such a church is ministering in an outward direction to those who have not yet been reconciled to their loving heavenly Father. And the missional church is ministering in an inward direction to help believers know Christ better. Subsequently, missional is not just ministering out, it is ministering in too.

A new name is needed that reminds the church of the necessity of inward and outward ministry balance.[3] Before we settle on a term, let's look at figure 7.1 to evaluate some customary terms and note their pros and cons in describing this balance.

Figure 7.1

CHURCH LABELS[4]				
Name	History	Pros	Cons	Balance between Outward and Inward Focus
Traditional Church (1770s–today)	Historical mainline congregations[5]	Historical and stable	May be captive to tradition	Inward leaning toward preserving organization and tradition
Holiness Churches (1860s–today)	Opposed slavery and broke with traditional churches at the time of the Civil War[6]	Emphasize walk the walk if you talk the talk	Outward behaviors are sometimes scrutinized to ascertain holiness	Outward and inward leaning in the 1800s toward both mercy ministry and holiness
				Inward leaning in the twentieth century toward developing personal signs of holiness
Social Gospel Churches (1910s–today)	Emphasizes meeting the needs of the poor (among other things)[7]	Mercy ministries help the needy	Meeting physical needs may take precedence over spiritual needs	Outward leaning with mercy ministries toward the non-churchgoing needy

continued

Figure 7.1 *continued*

CHURCH LABELS				
Name	**History**	**Pros**	**Cons**	**Balance between Outward and Inward Focus**
Pentecostal or Charismatic Churches (1910s–today)	Emphasizes a visible sign of sanctification, customarily speaking in tongues or other super-natural gifts[8]	Stresses discipleship since everyone has spiritual gifts to discover and utilize	Conversion can take a secondary emphasis to seeking spiritual gifts	Inward leaning toward helping Christians already converted to experience deeper spiritual experiences
Evangelical Churches (1950s–today)	Designation for churches emphasizing a born-again conversion experience[9]	Emphasis upon conversion	Mercy ministries that lead up to conversion may be neglected	Outward and inward leaning, but mostly in the narrow period just before or right after a person's conversion

While each of these categories is valid, all are somewhat imbalanced in their inward and outward focus. In his very last instructions to his disciples, Jesus put it differently. He gave them a tri-fold vision for ministry, not only to the new converts assembled there but to people nearby and even in far-flung locales, saying, "You will receive power when the Holy Spirit has come upon you, and you will be my witnesses in Jerusalem, in all Judea and Samaria, and to the end of the earth" (Acts 1:8 CEB).[10]

A Term Is Needed That Emphasizes a Church's Global Focus

Some churches, like the one in the example that began this chapter, take Jesus' admonition and focus on the last phrase, "to the ends of the earth" (Acts 1:8). Jesus was reminding his hearers that their mission and ministry was not confined to the people assembled in Jerusalem that day. His intention was that the good news should keep spreading to every corner and hamlet on the globe. First it would spread across the Jewish homeland of Judea. Then it would leap the cultural gap between the Jews and the Samaritans next door, against whom many Jews were bigoted. By including the Samaritans, Jesus emphasized that his church is called to minister not just locally, but also across cultural chasms to bring both spiritual and physical reconciliation.

The allure of "to the ends of the earth" often makes mission work next door seem mundane and uninspiring. And because of the stark need in many developing countries (as well as perhaps an exotic allure), churches can become imbalanced, focusing on foreign needs and ignoring those that are local.[11] So many churches inadvertently create an imbalance by focusing on needs in exotic locales and ignoring the needs next door. (Refer back to David McKenna's quote that began this chapter.)

A Term Is Needed That Emphasizes a Church's Local Focus

Though the tendency may be for churches to focus on foreign locales, there are other churches that observe the needs of those next door and focus on them. (Categories of these churches were explored in figure 7.1.)

> The closer nonchurchgoers live to a church, the more they will expect that church to help them when they are in need.

Local residents may actually have a heightened expectation that a local church will help them. I have found in my consulting interviews that the closer in proximity nonchurchgoers live to a church, the more they will expect that church to help them when they are in need. One neighborhood resident put it this way, "They [the churchgoers nearby] always show up with their fancy cars, park in my parking spot, and just kind of ignore that we live here. And when I tried to get some help for our grand-daughter, they told me about some program downtown. They are right in my neighborhood, and they don't even notice or care about my needs." This and similar responses I have received may indicate that people right next door to your church are expecting your church to be their first resource in times of calamity or want.

A Term Is Needed That Emphasizes a Church's Glocal Focus

In an attempt to describe organizations involved both locally and globally, a new term was championed by British sociologist Rolland Robertson: *glocal* which combines *global* with *local*.[12] A host of Christian books have followed suit, using *glocal* as a descriptor for a congregation that is engaged in local and global ministry.[13]

I have noticed a problem when the term *glocal* is applied to churches. It underemphasizes the needs of the congregants. Usually, Christian authors use *glocal* in a way that calls attention to reaching nonchurchgoers, both locally and globally.[14] But the fellowship of believers has needs too (though it must be remembered they pale in comparison to the spiritual needs of those who do not yet know Christ). As the story that began this chapter illustrated, a congregation must be healthy if it is to meet the needs of nonchurchgoers.

Therefore, a term more inclusive than *glocal* is needed. A term is required which reminds us that meeting the needs of nonchurchgoers locally and globally also requires sustaining and assisting the health of a congregation of believers.

A Term That Emphasizes a Church's Conglocal Focus May Be the Answer

Even from the short overview in figure 7.1, it is easy to see that a term is needed that can remind churches of their need to balance congregational, local, and global ministries.[15] *Conglocal* may be the term that describes this triune nature of the church. Figure 7.2 offers a definition, and figure 7.3 explains the derivation of the term in much the same fashion as sociologist Rolland Robertson created *glocal*.

Figure 7.2

DEFINITION OF A CONGLOCAL CHURCH
A conglocal church is a congregation that has a balanced three-fold heart for foreign missions, local missions, and congregants.

Figure 7.3

THE DEVELOPMENT OF THE TERM *CONGLOCAL*
• *Con*gregation—emphasizing the church is meeting the needs of the congregation • *Glo*bal—emphasizing the church is also meeting the spiritual and physical needs of people globally • Lo*cal*—emphasizing the church is meeting the spiritual and physical needs of local residents • *Conglocal*—a conglocal church demonstrates a balanced three-fold heart for local, global, and congregational health and mission.

PRINCIPLES OF THE CONGLOCAL CHURCH

Picturing Conglocal Balance for Meeting Congregational, Local, and Global Needs

The designation *conglocal* reminds a congregation that it must balance its ministry to those inside the congregation, those nearby who are outside of it, and those who are far away. In my consulting work, I have noticed that many churches spend the majority of their time looking after and meeting the needs of those within the congregation. This arises because the needs of those inside the congregation are heard the loudest and most frequently due to social proximity.

But the needs of those inside the congregation pale in comparison with those outside the church. One writer starkly reminds us, "When a person dies without hearing that ['God so loved the world that he gave his one and only Son, that whoever believes in him shall

Figure 7.4

THE CONGLOCAL HEART OF A CONGREGATION

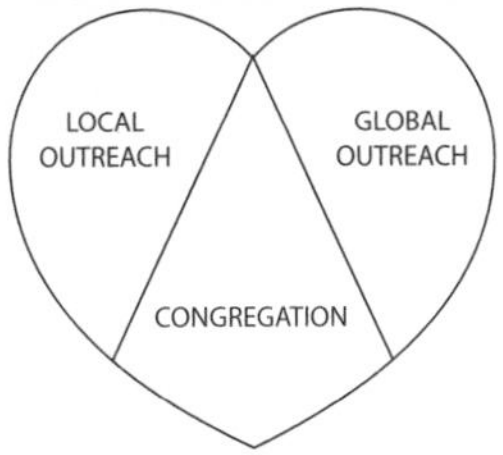

not perish but have eternal life' (John 3:16)], it is too late. The best thing that could possibly happen to that person has been denied."[16]

To help visualize this three-fold heart for congregational, local, and global needs, the church can be pictured as a three-chambered heart (see figure 7.4).

In figure 7.4, congregational needs create a foundation, depicted in the lower section of the heart. Such placement is not to suggest primacy, but only to remind us that a foundation of health can better help a congregation minister to others locally and globally.

Conglocal Balance in Your Financial Expenditures

A key element of balanced conglocal ministry is balancing your fiscal expenditures in each category. In one client church, the pastor stood and boldly proclaimed that the church was now giving 20 percent of its income to local (10 percent) and global (10 percent) ministries. While this is a step in the right direction, the church's lavish marble atrium reminded visitors that 80 percent of this congregation's income was still spent upon itself.

If churches are to foster authentic reconciliation between haves and have-nots as well as across physical chasms, then churches must start balancing their spending. The conglocal model provides a visual cue to a church's three-fold fiscal obligations. In a church with a growing conglocal heart, you will find an increased balance of expenditures toward meeting the needs of not just congregants, but also the local and global communities.

> The conglocal model provides a visual cue to a church's three-fold fiscal obligations.

Conglocal Balance in Your Church Life

More than balancing need-meeting in financial expenditures, it is important to balance your fellowship congregationally, locally, and globally. Most churches spend a great deal of their time getting to know the needs of those within the congregation. Though there is nothing wrong with this, it can often be out of balance. A congregation must also regularly share life and inter-action with those who don't attend their church and those who don't live nearby.

Research shows that face-to-face encounters help people from different cultures and socioeconomic levels accept and support one another.[17] Such face-to-face encounters with local and global people who don't attend your church is an important tactic to maintain a conglocal balance. Still, some members may say that they work forty-plus hours a week with nonchurchgoers and question if this is sufficient. Regrettably, in most of those workplace interactions, there is very little sharing of spiritual values. Plus in many workplaces, discussing spiritual beliefs is discouraged. The conglocal church intentionally creates opportunities for local and global nonchurchgoers to graciously discuss their faith journeys.

For example, one church cancelled its Sunday morning service, telling its congregants to go into the community to "find a need and fill it." The pastor's intention was to get the congregants out into the community, seeking to understand and meet the needs of nonchurchgoers. That Sunday, hundreds of congregants spread out across the city to meet needs in Jesus' name.

While sharing this story at a seminar, I noticed the assembled Wesleyan pastors looked uncomfortable. General Superintendent of The Wesleyan Church, Dr. Jo Anne Lyon, was seated behind me as I spoke. At the end my seminar, she took the podium and addressed my puzzlement over the reaction of the pastors. "I know why some of you were uncomfortable with the idea of canceling church and going out to serve the community," Dr. Lyon began. "I know it is because if you did, you couldn't count those people in your monthly attendance totals. Now, I don't know if I have authority to do this. But I'm going to go ahead and say that if you send your people out to serve nonchurchgoers on a Sunday, then you can count every person they touch has having been in Jesus' presence that day." Kindhearted smiles swept across the seminar participants, as they recognized that this general superintendent would not let customs stand in the way of reaching out to those in need.

EXERCISES TO CREATE CONGLOCAL ENGAGEMENT

Overcoming Your Discomfort (Intimacy)

Exercise Plan. Recall a time when you encountered a different culture, then answer the following questions: Did you feel uncomfortable? Why? What should you do about that? What needs did you see in that different culture that you feel you may have been able to meet? When you encounter that culture next time, what will you do differently?

Variations. Vary the cultures that you recall. For generational cultures, recall someone who was much older than you and to whom you found it hard to relate. Ask yourself the above questions about that encounter. Another option is to recall encounters with affinity groups, such as people from a different socioeconomic status or interest or hobby. Again, ask the same questions. Frequently repeating this exercise and using varying cultures can help you overcome your discomfort to see needs you can meet.

Principles. Having face-to-face (and eventually heart-to-heart) interaction with those who are unlike you can help you see past your discomfort and discover their needs.

Take the Good News Out to Where They Are (Intimacy)

Exercise Plan. Recall a time when you were not in church on a Sunday morning but instead out in the secular community. If that has been a while, make arrangements to attend church at another time so you can spend a Sunday morning observing what takes place among those who do not attend church.

Then answer the following questions: How large were the crowds you encountered? What kind of people where they? Were some different than you? Were some similar to you? Do you think many of them regularly attend church? Why or why not? If you had thirty seconds to tell them about your church, what would you say?

Variations. Share your thirty-second church description and ask for corrections or suggestions from two people who are part of your church and two people who are not part (as far as you know) of any faith community. Rewrite your thirty-second church description, keep it with you, and share it when the opportunity arises.

Principles. As Jesus came into our world and took on the very nature of a servant to communicate with us (Rom. 2:5–8), so too churchgoers must regularly and repeatedly venture out into the non-churchgoing world to serve and share.

Adopting Those in Need (Impact)

Submitted by Joel Liechty, student, Wesley Seminary at Indiana Wesleyan University, Marion, Indiana; Jay Height, pastor, Shepherd Community Center, Indianapolis, Indiana; and Adam Knight, lead pastor, University United Methodist Church (west campus), San Antonio, Texas.

Exercise Plan. Individuals and churches often valiantly give to the needy only to feel they are hardly making a dent in the need. Try giving up handing out money, food, and clothes, along with tutoring, mentoring, and health programs. Instead, start an "adopt a family program" where the church adopts three to five families a year and then meets all of their needs, including financial assistance, tutoring, counseling, food, and clothes. By focusing on a few families, the church can more thoroughly help a family break out of the poverty cycle. And each year more families are adopted.

Variations. A similar "adopt a family program" can be utilized with churches and even foreign mission projects. College students have adopted villages in Haiti under the DecAid Project, agreeing that for ten years they will meet all of the needs of those villagers that cannot meet their own needs.[18] And suburban churches are adopting "sister congregations" in urban communities to share their wealth, assets, and volunteer base.[19] Still other suburban churches are partnering with urban congregations to cohost block parties and festivals in local parks.

Principles. The principle of welcoming those in need into our family is found in the Old Testament story of Ruth and Naomi, as well as in Paul's reminder that God has adopted us so that we can now even call him "Abba, Father" (Rom. 8:15). The psalmist said it poetically: "Father of orphans, champion of widows, is God in his holy house. God makes homes for the homeless [and] leads prisoners to freedom" (Ps. 68:5–6 MSG).

Serve Locally by Linking Small Groups (Impact)

Exercise Plan. Part of conglocal ministry is not overlooking local needs. To increase local outreach, link together two to five small groups to better serve the community. By linking small groups, you not only foster intergroup fellowship, but also garner enough people-power to accomplish the sometimes daunting tasks of serving nonchurchgoers.

For example, two Sunday school classes can join together and visit a local soup kitchen or community center on Saturday morning to serve meals. The Sunday school groups could then meet the next day (Sunday) and draft a list of seven things that surprised them and three things Christians could do to help people at the soup kitchen. The combined groups could also create steps to guide other Sunday school classes in a similar outreach. The combined groups could then schedule a time during an upcoming church service to share their ideas. The Christian education director (or another church leader) would oversee the pairing of two more classes or groups. This new group goes out and undertakes a similar service during next quarter. This new grouping also creates a list of seven surprises and three action steps, sharing this on a Sunday morning too. Other groups in the church would be encouraged to join together to meet the needs of unchurched people. A Christian education volunteer would be a suitable person to oversee this.

Variations. Groups do not need to be comprised of Sunday school classes; any church group can be utilized. Try pairing the board of trustees with the worship team or a prayer group with the ushers. Get creative and connect disparate groups together. As they serve nonchurchgoers together, they will most likely forget about any trivial differences.

Principles. This exercise takes people from dissimilar groups in a church and requires them to work together for a common goal. It takes the focus off of their own needs and wants (which often is what causes division) and places them on a common cause: others.

Local Study Tour (Impact)

Submitted by Adam Knight, lead pastor, University United Methodist Church (west campus), San Antonio, Texas.

Exercise Plan. Set congregational study groups in missionally appropriate places outside of your church. One church is working to develop a confirmation curriculum that is not set inside the church. Instead, each session meets at a different location in town to illustrate the point. For instance, on the night the church will talk about the incarnation of Christ, the class might meet at an inner-city mission house, where a group of people have committed to intentionally live among the poor and disenfranchised they are trying to reach. On the night the church will discuss the understanding of personal holiness, people might meet at an area monastery to discuss spiritual disciplines. And for the discussion of social holiness, people might meet at a local soup kitchen. The goal is to allow the setting to teach as much as the content.

Variations. You can visit similar locales as appropriate. For instance, have a study on healing inside the local hospital, do a study of evangelism in a local coffee house or bar. This exercise can also be expanded on occasion to global sites.

Principles. This exercise stresses that faith (and the elements that make up our faith) don't just happen inside a church building, but increase in relevance as they occur in the world.

EIGHT

THE CHURCH AND SPIRITUAL TRANSFORMATION

EXERCISES IN NEW LIFE

What we see is that anyone united with the Messiah
gets a fresh start, is created new. The old life is gone;
a new life burgeons! Look at it!

—2 Corinthians 5:17 MSG

A STILL SMALL VOICE

"I'm a little nervous," confided Jenny as she looked at the
audience. "I don't have a story like Scott. Will they accept it?"

"Sure they will," came a friend's sympathetic reply. "My story
was not like Scott's either."

Over the next ten minutes, Jenny shared a story of faith and
transformation. The event was hosted by Jenny's church as a
quarterly celebration of lives that were transformed by Christ.
Scott's story, which preceded hers, seemed to be the most
noteworthy. A tale of drug abuse and cutting himself, Scott's

troubled family life had made him despondent and suicidal. But a personal encounter with Jesus had sent Scott in a new direction. His story was moving, inspirational . . . and, for Jenny, formidable.

In contrast Jenny had experienced none of the overt rebellion of Scott. Hers was the story of a girl raised in a Christian home who struggled with bulimia. Though initially she struggled to gain her composure in front of the audience, Jenny slowly but steadily increased in clarity. "It finally came to suicide," summed up Jenny. "I was on the verge of doing it. But then I met David. He explained that only God had the strength to help me break with my past. He told me about people like Scott, who had overcome what seemed like so much more. David just made it seem plausible that God wanted a better life for me. He made it clear that through Jesus' sacrifice, I had a route back to a heavenly Father who had a purpose for me."

Afterward, a crowd of teens gathered around the speakers. Around Scott was a sizable crowd of boys and girls. Jenny didn't expect anyone to take much notice of her less-colorful story. But soon a throng nearly the size of Scott's crowd, and mostly young girls, gathered around her. "You gave me a voice," said one. "I can talk about my eating disorder now. I felt like you too. I wanted to die. But in your story I can see my answer."

For the next twenty minutes, Jenny shared, counseled, consoled, and prayed with the young women in her circle. "I'm so glad the church did this," shared Jenny later.

"Did what?" I asked.

"Gave voice to what God has done . . . and will do."

THE POWER OF NEW LIFE

A New Way of Living and Dying

There are many ways to define an experience of new life. When someone starts over in a new town or with a new job, people may say he or she has begun a new life. But the new life that Christ offers is much more.

Christ offers a transformation that launches humans in a new spiritual and physical direction (Gal. 5:22–25). This transformation involves the emergence of a new lifestyle that is focused on putting others ahead of ourselves (Mark 9:35; James 1:26–27), with a new forgiveness of and hope for humanity (Matt. 5:1–16) and an expectation of eternity (John 5:24; 1 John 5:13). And though the task seems daunting, God promises to empower us to meet the challenge to live this new life (Acts 1:8; 2 Cor. 12:9; Phil. 4:13).

New Life as Conversion

Conversion is the common term to describe this amazing and magnificent experience. In popular culture, this term is often applied with a more cynical tone. The coercive nature of "forced conversions" both religiously[1] and politically[2] have clouded the original biblical intent. And when used in a legal sense, *conversion* means the illegal acquisition of someone else's property. Even a quick Internet search for the term *conversion* brings up (in this order) conversion of measurements, legal definitions, atrocities of forced conversions, and then only somewhat later, religious conversion.[3]

Mixed connotations associated with conversion make the use of a more relevant and up-to-date term attractive. The most straightforward phrase may be to describe the new life in Christ as a spiritual and physical transformation.

New Life as Spiritual and Physical Transformation

The term *spiritual transformation* signifies an inward character change that creates a new inner self and perspective, and *physical transformation* reminds us that this spiritual transformation will be accompanied by behavioral changes as well. Figure 8.1 provides a brief comparison of some of the transformations that can occur before and after new life.

Figure 8.1

EXAMPLES OF TRANSFORMATION BEFORE AND AFTER NEW LIFE		
Before Transformation	**What Changed?**	**After Transformation**
You meet your own needs first (Gal. 5:19–21).	Self	You meet the needs of others first (Mark 9:35; Gal. 5:13).
Your sin separates you from a sinless God (Isa. 59:2).	Sin	God forgives your sin and restores you to fellowship with him (Rom. 3:23–24).
You must work hard for brief periods of tranquility (Ps. 127:1).	Tranquility	God gives a peace that is beyond what you can muster yourself (Phil. 4:7; Heb. 6:19).
Your life is characterized by strife, worry, envy, and lust (James 4:1–2).	Outward appearance	Your life is characterized by love, joy, peace, and patience (Gal. 5:22–23).
Eternal life holds eternal judgment (2 Thess. 1:9).	Eternity	Eternal life holds a new realm of peace and serenity (Gal. 6:7–8).

PRINCIPLES OF NEW LIFE

How Does Transformation Happen?

In order to understand this marvelous intersection of the supernatural and the natural, let's define what spiritual and physical transformation looks like in figure 8.2.

Figure 8.2

DEFINING SPIRITUAL AND PHYSICAL TRANSFORMATION (CONVERSION)
When repentance is combined with faith, it brings about spiritual and physical transformation.[4]

Repentance. The customary biblical word for repentance is *metanoia*, meaning "a change of mind" that arises out of "remorse (as regret for short comings and errors)."[5] It "conveys the idea of turning, but focuses on the inner, cognitive decision to make a break with the past."[6] This happens when people are not satisfied with life's direction and want to break with the past. *Metanoia* therefore reminds us that new life begins with an emerging dissatisfaction. This growing dissatisfaction can be depicted as a series of stages, or spiritual waypoints, in a person's spiritual journey to Christ (figure 8.3).

Figure 8.3

SPIRITUAL WAYPOINTS LEADING UP TO REPENTANCE[7]
Waypoint
14. Initial awareness of the good news
13. Awareness of the fundamentals of the good news
12. Grasp of the implications of the good news
11. Positive attitude toward the good news
10. Personal problem recognition
9. Decision to act
8. Repentance and faith in Christ
7. New birth

Faith. *Pistis* is the New Testament Greek word meaning "faith [and] trust."[8] Robert Coleman reminds us that everyone has a "common faith" without which it would be impossible to live, for "common faith . . . comes in driving a car on a busy highway. . . . You must have an incredible amount of faith in those strangers who speed by you. Yet without that trust, you could never drive a car."[9] However, transformational faith (see Heb. 1:1; 11:6) conveys a "faith, trust, [and] confidence in God" that he wants to help you change for the better and has the power to help you do so.[10]

Spiritual and Physical Transformation. The term in the New Testament for transformation is *epistrophe*, meaning "to turn around" and to have "a change of mind . . . [to turn] from something to something [else]."[11] It is literally a "reversing direction and going the opposite way."[12] Such a turnaround emerges from a series of spiritual life phases (as seen in figure 8.3). Some biblical passages that give insight into the magnitude of this change include 1 Corinthians 6:9–11; Matthew 8:2–4; and Acts 3:19.

Who Accomplishes This Transformation, and What Exactly Is It?

A temptation is to think that by hard work and diligence alone we can accomplish this transition ourselves. A parallel temptation is to think the exercises in this book will empower us to muster this transformation. But this transformation is so deeply inward and outward that it can only come from the One who created us. Here is how Romans 3:23–24 puts it: "Since we've compiled this long and sorry record as sinners (both us and them) and proved that we are utterly incapable of living the glorious lives God wills for us, God did it for us. Out of sheer generosity he put us in right standing with himself. A pure gift. He got us out of the mess we're in and restored us to where he always wanted us to be. And he did it by means of Jesus Christ" (MSG).

An updated definition of *conversion*, in figure 8.4, adds the new insights we have gleaned from understanding the terms *repentance*, *faith*, and *spiritual and physical transformation.*

Figure 8.4

UPDATED DEFINITION OF CONVERSION	
Repentance	When remorse for the things we have done makes us want to break with the past . . .
Faith	. . . combined with trust and confidence that God wants to help us change and has the power to help us do so . . .
Spiritual and Physical Transformation	. . . then by God's sovereign work in Jesus Christ, a change in human direction occurs toward a never-ending life of serving others and sharing this good news.

When Does Transformation Happen?

Because spiritual and physical transformation is a miraculous intersection of the divine and the natural, it is not surprising that it takes place in a personalized manner for almost everyone. Jesus explained it this way: "Don't be so surprised when I tell you that you have to be 'born from above' — out of this world, so to speak. You know well enough how the wind blows this way and that. You hear it rustling through the trees, but you have no idea where it comes from or where it's headed next. That's the way it is with everyone 'born from above' by the wind of God, the Spirit of God" (John 3:7–8 MSG).

Suddenly, at Once.[13] Often people describe their conversion as sudden. It may commence with "a sudden point-in-time transformation based on an encounter with Jesus."[14] Such was Paul's experience on the road to Damascus in Acts 9. Today in many evangelical churches, this may be the way that conversion is commonly expected.[15]

Gradually, Over Time. In Scripture we also see this transformation taking place slowly. Jesus' analogy to the varying and mysterious ways of the wind emphasizes this (John 3:8). For some, like many of the apostles and as exemplified by Simon Peter, transformation appears to have taken place gradually.[16]

There was no point or event where we see the "eureka" factor in Peter, much less most of the other disciples.[17] Their transformations seemed to take place gradually. And though such gradual transformation may be less celebrated in evangelical churches,[18] psychologist Lewis Rambo believes gradual conversion may be the most common experience of Christians. Rambo summarized, "For the most part it (religious conversion) takes place over a period of time."[19]

> As the church, we must be more aware of God's fondness for variety.

Therefore, it may be best to let the Holy Spirit blow as he wishes. The mysterious and manifold ways that the Holy Spirit transforms humans is not just declared in John 3:8, but also evident in history from New Testament times until today. As the church, we must be more aware of God's fondness for variety. The following exercises were created to help churches recall and regularly experience God's marvelous and varied work in spiritual and physical transformation.

EXERCISES TO EXPERIENCE NEW LIFE[20]

My Road to Transformation (Intimacy)

Exercise Plan. Recall a time when you underwent a spiritual and physical transformation. (The purpose here is to write out your journey to Christ, noting specific spiritual changes that you have experienced since he transformed you. However, don't dwell on any one era too extensively. Rather, write your narrative in such a way that you cover most of the major spiritual periods you have gone through.) What feelings did you have before this occurred? Was there a rising dissatisfaction in your life and a desire to "make a break with the past"?[21]

The Greek word for repentance (*metanoia*) reminds us that this new life begins with an emerging dissatisfaction. Describe in a short sentence or two how you worked through this dissatisfaction. If the results are not too personal, share them with a group of close friends.

When did you become aware of the fundamentals of the good news? When did you fully understand the implications of the good news for you? When did you have a positive attitude toward the good news? When was the first time you discovered a rising dissatisfaction with a personal problem and desired to make a break with your past? Did you make a decision to act? Have you repented and put your faith in Christ? Have you experienced new birth?

Variations. There are other depictions that map out the spiritual journey, such as Engel's scale of spiritual decision.[22] Use one of these questions in lieu of the questions above if you find them more relevant.

When were you first aware of a Supreme Being but had no knowledge of the gospel? When was your first awareness of the gospel? Are you aware of the fundamentals of the gospel? Do you currently grasp the implications of the gospel? Do you have a positive attitude toward the gospel? Have you ever had a personal problem in recognizing the value of the gospel? When was your decision to act and accept Christ? Can you verbalize your story of repentance and faith in Christ?

Principles. The purpose of this exercise is to help a person see that the transformative experience is a varied and often progressive process. This not only helps people see how far they have come, but also gives them hope as they observe God's provision in the past.

My Transformation: Sudden or Slow (Intimacy)

Exercise Plan. Recall the time when you first knew that a spiritual and physical transformation had begun in you. Read Acts 9, and tell how your conversion was similar to or different from Paul's.

Look at these stories from Peter's life, and tell how your experience was different or similar: Matthew 16:13–20; 26:69–75; Acts 2:14–47.

Variations. Read the conversion stories of well-known Christians. Then divide a sheet of paper into three columns. In the left column, list how your transformation was similar to the ones you read about. In the middle column, list how your transformation was different. And in the right column, write any lessons you learned.

Principles. The purpose is to see that God sometimes works quickly (to save us from a colossal misstep, such as Paul heading to Damascus to imprison Christians there), and at other times he transforms people slowly (most of Jesus' disciples). By creating a congregational expectation for God's Holy Spirit to blow quickly into some lives while gently into others', a congregation begins to welcome the various ways and speeds in which God transforms people.

How I Have Changed (Intimacy)

Exercise Plan. Look back at figure 8.1. For each box in the left column, write one paragraph describing your life before transformation. Then for each box in the right column, write one paragraph describing your life after transformation. What does this tell you about how much and to what extent you have changed? Write a summary paragraph and put this summation in your Bible next to 2 Corinthians 5:17.

Variations. Undertake the same exercise, but instead of using figure 8.1, write a paragraph about the two different ways of living (deeds of the flesh and fruit of the Spirit) in Galatians 5:16–26.

Principles. The lesson here is that though we may be struggling with becoming more like Christ, he has already significantly transformed us from the selfish interests that controlled our previous lives. Paul, no stranger to a momentous transformation, put it this way: "Don't be deceived. Those who are sexually immoral, those who worship false gods, adulterers, both participants in same-sex intercourse, thieves, the greedy, drunks, abusive people, and swindlers won't inherit God's kingdom. That is what some of you used to be! But you were washed clean, you were made holy to God, and you were made right with God in the name of the Lord Jesus Christ and in the Spirit of our God" (1 Cor. 6:9–11 CEB).

The Good News in Common Dress (Impact)

Exercise Plan. This is similar to what past Christians called a testimony service. The label may be antiquated, so "celebration of new life," "good news gathering," and "celebrating our faith journeys" have been used in recent years. Regardless of the title, the purpose is for Christians to explain briefly and in simple terms the story of how they became a Christian. This should take place at least once a year, and many churches have held this at a service the week before Thanksgiving.

The process includes a question that sets the stage and a time limit that regulates the length of the response (spiritual changes can be so profound for the person that they may take an inordinate amount of time to describe it). In addition a host who keeps any participants from lengthy stories is useful.

Variations. Ask variations on the question, but always try to ensure that it is relevant to people who have experienced gradual transformation as well as those who may have experienced sudden transformation. Vary the length each year to ensure the maximum amount of participants are involved and that narratives are not too long.

Principles. The key is for congregants of different ages, cultures, and social groups to observe Christ moving in the hearts and lives of ages, cultures, and social groups that are different from their own. Paul summed it up this way:

> Scripture reassures us, "No one who trusts God like this — heart and soul — will ever regret it." It's exactly the same no matter what a person's religious background may be: the same God for all of us, acting the same incredibly generous way to everyone who calls out for help. "Everyone who calls, 'Help, God!' gets help. But how can people call for help if they don't know who to trust? And how can they know who to trust if they haven't heard of the One who can be trusted? And how can they hear if nobody tells them? And how is anyone going to tell them, unless someone is sent to do it? (Rom. 10:11–14 MSG)

Meeting Needs During Life Transitions (Impact)

Submitted by Charles "Chip" Arn, author, professor, and researcher on church outreach, Glendora, California.

Exercise Plan. Significant changes in people's lifestyles often cause them to ask spiritual questions. Such events may be controlled events (marriage, divorce, relocation, retirement) or uncontrolled events (death of a spouse, medical crisis, termination of employment). Encourage congregants at the beginning of Lent (or at any other time of the year) to be aware of transitional events of those in their social network and to respond in genuine Christian love and help.

Variations. Church ministry leaders can refocus ministry programs or begin new ones to share God's unconditional love with people whom God may be preparing for the spiritual transformation they and he desires.

Principles. Jesus spoke of this principle when he told his disciples to turn their eyes upon the vast fields of human souls that were seeking God and to note that they were already "ripe for harvest" (John 4:35). He also described how they should plant seeds of his good news in good (receptive) soil (Matt. 13:1–9) and to preach in the communities that are interested and amenable (Luke 9:1–6). How do you identify the receptive people in your community? One way is through life-transformation events.

NINE

HOW TO CUSTOMIZE THE EXERCISES FOR YOUR CHURCH

IDEA GENERATORS FOR INTIMACY AND IMPACT

The exercises in the previous pages have been selected from my consulting observations as well as from submissions from colleagues, students, and fellow researchers.[1] These exercises are listed here, not as end-all or be-all exercises, but rather as thought provokers and idea generators to help you create and combine them into new exercises that are right for you and your congregation.

Each chapter's exercises also address two parallel themes: developing personal intimacy with God as well as creating impact upon others regarding that theme. Let's briefly review the two types of exercises contained in each chapter.

Intimacy Exercises. To ensure that each chapter does not only address church-wide attitudes and overlook personal needs for emotional health, the first exercises in each chapter are focused on helping the reader develop intimacy with God on that chapter's topic.

Impact Exercises. The next exercises in each chapter are designed to get an entire congregation (or a portion of it, such as a team, sub-congregation, or small group) developing their communal heart health.[2]

FOUR STEPS TO CUSTOMIZING THESE EXERCISES

The Collaborative Power of Improvisation[3]

Many exercises in this book are not yet ideal for your situation. Instead, use them as idea generators and fundamental concepts from which to grow custom exercises that are right for you. To visualize this customization, I will employ the term and imagery of theater *improvisation* (sometimes shortened to *improv*).

> Improvisation, whether in a theatre or in customizing these exercises, requires a planning process with four steps.

When the word *improv* is used, many people often think of unplanned, sketch comedy. But improvisation actually requires a planning process with four steps. To adapt these exercises into something more helpful for the reader's local situation, follow these four steps of improvisation.

Step 1: Choose an Exercise. Improvisation must start somewhere. In theatrical improvisation, an idea is tossed to the actors, usually from the audience. In our improvisation, creative ideas will be tossed to you from the exercises in this book. Therefore:

- Read all the exercises in a chapter.
- Look for common threads running through these exercises and write them down and use them to guide your improv.
- Select an exercise that by mutual agreement seems the most appealing and helpful.

Step 2: Don't Block, Add! The next step is to add local color to your exercise. This is one of the most logical but often one of the most overlooked steps. To accomplish this, use the principle of "Don't block, add."[4] This means any new idea should build upon the previous concept and localize it. This "don't block, add" is a key principle of improvisation.

My son-in-law teaches theatre improvisation and once told me, "When a person says, 'I'm a tree,' then the next person should *never* say, 'No, you are not a tree. You are a bird.' That would be called 'blocking,' for you are blocking the previous person's idea or action. Instead, always agree with the first person but then *add* your own idea to theirs."[5] Improvisation succeeds when you do not challenge the initial idea (which is called blocking[6]), but instead add your idea to the original concept to make it a team product.

Improvise the exercises in this book by taking the exercise you selected in step 1 above and begin adding elements to it. This is accomplished through the following:

- In a group setting, read aloud the exercise you selected in step 1.

- Everyone in the group should then add their ideas to make the exercise work better for the team.
- Focus on good ideas that will work for your group. This will usually eliminate weaker ones.
- Keep adding ideas to the mix.
- Before the exercise gets too complex, edit the exercise into something the team agrees will work.

Step 3: Try, Tweak, and See. Now it is time to try out an exercise, modify it as needed, and see if it works.

If an exercise is intended for an entire church or a large group, try it out first in a smaller setting. Trying a new exercise with a large group often results in public failure, which can thwart future heart exercises in this area. Rather, test out your idea in smaller and friendlier confines. Oftentimes this can be among the leadership team itself or a volunteer small group.

Tweaking or modifying means that if the exercise needs to be changed some more, go ahead and do so. Then go back and try it again.

Finally, see how participants and observers feel about the exercise and adjust accordingly. Be sure to get feedback by asking participants to tell you what they learned from each exercise. Eliminate exercises that have little positive effect.

Step 4: Repeat Exercises That Work for You. Exercises do not strengthen a human body unless they are repeated. The same is true for the exercises in this book. Find the ones that work for your church and repeat them regularly. Here are a few suggested ways to accomplish this:

- Monthly exercise plan: Select one chapter per month and introduce an exercise from that chapter to your church.

- Retreat and advance: Use selected chapters from this book as the agenda for a leadership retreat. Break attendees into small groups and have each use the four steps of improvisation to customize an exercise for the church. At the end of the retreat have a competition, ranking the customized exercises on creativity, impact, and intimacy. Of course, be careful not to deride any exercises, but rather look for strengths in each. Oftentimes exercises that are less effective can be combined to form a hybrid exercise.

- Personal exercise regimen: Use this book's intimacy exercises once a month as a devotional in addition to or in lieu of your regular devotional agenda. This can help build personal heart strength while also adding variety to your devotional life.

- A small group exercise regimen: This is a variation of the personal regimen (above). To undertake a group version, semi-regularly replace your Sunday school, small group, or Bible study curriculum with a chapter from this book. Leaders can select chapter topics that are appropriate for the group's heart health.

Keep a Journal of Health Exercises

Use a journal, such as the example in figure 9.1 to track progress and improvise new exercises that are right for you. Figure 9.1 will also help you regularly improvise more intimacy and impact exercises from the examples in each chapter.

As you continue tracking, improvising, and adapting the exercises in this book, you will experience heart health that is relevant, productive, and enjoyable. But the best outcome is not only that you are exercising your way back to personal spiritual health and a spiritually healthy church, but that others are joining you on the journey.

Figure 9.1

HEART HEALTH JOURNAL		
Improv Step	**Directions**	**Notes**
1: Choose an Exercise	1. Read the exercises in a chapter. 2. Pick one exercise to start.	
2: Don't Block, Add!	1. Read aloud the original exercise. 2. Add ideas that would make it work better for you. 3. Ignore ideas that don't work. 4. Keep adding good ideas (and ignoring bad ideas).	
3: Try, Tweak, and See	1. Try out an exercise. If an exercise is intended for an entire church or a large group, try it out first in a smaller setting. 2. Tweak (modify) if needed. 3. See how you, participants, and observers feel about the exercise.	
4: Repeat Exercises That Work	1. Create a statement telling how and when you will repeat these exercises. 2. Write out, sign, and date this commitment.	

NOTES

Introduction

1. For applicability and anonymity, the illustrations that begin each chapter have been created from the stories of several clients. To respect confidentiality, names have been changed.

2. While emotions technically arise from a complex synergy between our brains and bodies, the metaphor of the heart as the center of human emotions has been around so long that it is widely accepted as a figure of speech.

3. Duke University, "American Congregations at the Beginning of the 21st Century," National Congregations Study, accessed September 10, 2012, http://www.soc.duke.edu/natcong/Docs/NCSII_report_final.pdf, 3.

4. David T. Olsen, *The American Church in Crisis: Groundbreaking Research Based on a National Database of over 200,000 Churches* (Grand Rapids, Mich.: Zondervan, 2008), 8, 37.

5. Reconnecting humans with their loving heavenly Father is the essence of the *missio Dei*, God's mission. I have found it helpful to describe the *missio Dei* and churches that participate in it this way: A missional church implies a congregation that participates daily in helping people reconnect with the loving heavenly Father who created them. For more information, see John Flett, *The Witness of God: The Trinity, Missio Dei, Karl Barth, and the Nature of Christian Community* (Grand Rapids, Mich.: Eerdmans, 2010).

6. For more on the distinction between a common church and the uncommonly healthy one that God desires, see Bob Whitesel, *Cure for the Common Church: God's Plan to Restore Church Health* (Indianapolis, Ind.: Wesleyan Publishing House, 2012). This present book follows and expands the themes begun in *Cure for the Common Church*.

Chapter One

1. I am not suggesting that the New Testament authors had ecclesial exercises per se in mind. But I am suggesting that they used analogies with the human body to emphasize how a church functions. Therefore, it is in keeping with the principle to suggest that other functions our Creator formed in our bodies can have parallel analogies in the church. One such analogy is exercise and its role in church health.

2. Eddie Gibbs, *Body Building Exercises for the Local Church* (London: Falcon, 1979), 39.

3. Mayo Clinic, *Mayo Clinic Fitness for Everybody* (Rochester, Minn.: Mayo Clinic, 2005), 2.

4. Unfortunately, most people (like most organizations) put exercise out of their minds until their health is so impaired and they must exercise or die. And for some it may be too little, too late. Though later is better than never, the person or organization wanting to prevent illness, while increasing energy and impact, will adopt an exercise regimen long before it is needed.

5. Bob Whitesel, *Growth By Accident, Death By Planning: How NOT to Kill a Growing Congregation* (Nashville: Abingdon, 2004); Bob Whitesel, *Organix: Signs of Leadership in a Changing Church* (Nashville: Abingdon, 2011); Bob Whitesel, *Preparing for Change Reaction: How to Introduce Change in Your Church* (Indianapolis, Ind.: Wesleyan Publishing House, 2007).

6. Charles Marsh and John M. Perkins, *Welcoming Justice: God's Movement toward Beloved Community* (Downers Grove, Ill.: InterVarsity Press 2009), 28–31.

7. John Perkins viewed the ultimate goal as a salvation experience and spiritual conversion like he had undergone. He now felt reconciled to his heavenly Father and emphasized that the most important of the Rs

was reconciliation (between God and humans and between humans and each other). But before this third R could be attained, Perkins believed the other two Rs often set the stage for spiritual transformation.

8. John M. Perkins, *A Quiet Revolution: The Christian Response to Human Need, a Strategy for Today* (Pasadena, Calif.: Urban Family Publications, 1976), 220.

9. This is not to say that churches with lower incomes should not participate in this kind of generosity. See how giving amid poverty is exemplified by the Macedonian church and lauded by Paul in 2 Corinthians 8:1–4.

10. A church would not be concerned only with its own needs, but it would partner with other churches to meet the needs of people from other cultures.

11. Tertullian, *The Apology* (39), quoted in Steven A. McKinion, ed., *Life and Practice in the Early Church: A Documentary Reader* (New York: New York University Press, 2001), 50.

Chapter Two

1. Personal conversation with author, May 6, 2005, Los Angeles, California. For more on Tribe of Los Angeles, see www.tribela.org.

2. It is important to remember that the church "partners" with God in his mission, and that the church does not itself do this mission. The reunification of humankind with the loving Father who created them is too grand and imposing a reconciliation for humans to accomplish. Only God is able to forge this restoration. Thus, the *missio Dei* is something only he can do. But he asks his offspring to participate. A church that participates effectively in this *missio Dei* is sometimes called a missional church and is involved in helping people reconnect with their loving Creator. When Christians offer physical or spiritual help in the name of a loving heavenly Father, they are helping reconnect with a loving Creator who is desperately seeking them. John Flett describes it this way: "The Father sent his Son and Spirit into the world, and this act reveals his 'sending' being. He remains active today in reconciling the world to himself and sends his community to participate in this mission" (John G. Flett, *The Witness of God: The Trinity,*

Missio Dei, Karl Barth, and the Nature of Christian Community [Grand Rapids, Mich.: Eerdmans, 2010], 5). And William Willimon says, "The church exists not for itself, but rather to sign, signal, and embody God's intentions for the whole world. God is going to get back what belongs to God. God's primary means of accomplishing this is through the church" (William H. Willimon, *Pastor: The Theology and Practice of Ordained Ministry* [Nashville: Abingdon, 2002], 240).

3. Elmer Towns, *10 of Today's Most Innovative Churches: What They're Doing, How They're Doing It, and How You Can Apply Their Ideas in Your Church* (Ventura, Calif.: Regal, 1991), 42–44.

4. A united church garners the watching world's respect, and this influence allows the church to point to the loving heavenly Father as the source of such unity and as one who wishes the same for them.

5. Tribe of Los Angeles exemplifies this. This church has created unity with an agape meal (communal meal and Communion) each Sunday before worship. I observed the pastor going to each person seated around the tables, serving Communion, and leading prayer time before the worship service commenced in another room. This and other activities created a bond in this congregation out of which grew new worship ideas that other churches around the nation began to adopt. (For more on this, see Bob Whitesel, *Inside the Organic Church: Learning from 12 Emerging Congregations* [Nashville: Abingdon, 2006], 98–107.) Though when I visited this church, there were fewer than fifty people, I found when I interviewed other innovative churches that they cited Tribe's congregation as a source of their inspiration. Tribe had an influence which belied its size. The worship leader at a midsized church told me Tribe had inspired him to adopt ideas about improvisational worship (worship leader, interview by Bob Whitesel, Solomon's Porch, Minneapolis, Minn., April 18, 2005). In my research, I have noticed that size is not necessarily linked to unity. But I have also observed that church unity is often linked to impact upon other congregations.

6. Towns, *Innovative Churches*, 79.

7. Bruno Dyck and Frederick A. Starke, "The Formation of Breakaway Organizations: Observations and a Process Model,"

Administrative Science Quarterly 44 (1999): 792–822; and Frederick A. Starke and Bruno Dyck, "Upheavals in Congregations: The Causes and Outcomes of Splits," *Review of Religious Research* 38 (1996): 159–174.

Chapter Three

1. For more on Herod's designation as "the Fox," see Leon Morris, *The Gospel According to Luke*, rep. ed. (Grand Rapids, Mich.: Eerdmans, 2002), 248–249.

2. William F. Arndt and F. Wilbur Gingrich, trans., *A Greek-English Lexicon of the New Testament and Other Early Literature* (Chicago: University of Chicago Press, 1957), 240–241.

3. The Great Commission is humanity's conscription into a participation in God's mission. In other words, humanity is called out to assist God in reconnecting with his wayward offspring. This is the essence of the *missio Dei* which was discussed in the introduction and chapter 1.

4. See Bob Whitesel, *Spiritual Waypoints: Helping Others Navigate the Journey* (Indianapolis, Ind.: Wesleyan Publishing House, 2010), 19; and Bob Whitesel, "Organizational Behavior: Grasping the Behavior and Personality of a Church," in *Foundations of Church Administration: Professional Tools for Church Leadership*, eds. Bruce L. Petersen, Edward A. Thomas, and Bob Whitesel (Kansas City, Mo.: Beacon Hill, 2010), 83–84.

5. It is interesting to note that Jesus put Leviticus 19:18 (a command to love your neighbor) as equal in force to Deuteronomy 6:5 (to love God). If you or I were doing this, we might be accused of equating two texts of differing weights. But Jesus, being the Son of God, has a right to do so, especially when he wished to stress to his church that linking love of God with love of neighbor has been his intention throughout history (which his church tends to repeatedly ignore).

6. Arndt and Gingrich, *Greek-English Lexicon*, 5–6; see also Edward Robinson, trans., *A Hebrew and English Lexicon of the Old Testament* (Oxford: Clarendon Press, 1974), 338–339.

7. Aleksandr I. Solzhenitsyn, *The Nobel Lecture on Literature* (New York: Harper & Row, 1972), 25.

8. Ibid.

9. Somaly Mam, *The Road of Lost Innocence: The True Story of a Cambodian Heroine* (New York: Spiegel & Grau, 2008), 193.

10. Michael Pocock, Gailyn Van Rheenen, and Douglas McConnell, *The Changing Face of World Missions: Engaging Contemporary Issues and Trends* (Grand Rapids, Mich.: Baker Academic, 2005), 65.

11. Anthony A. Hoekema, *Created in God's Image* (Grand Rapids, Mich.: Eerdmans, 1994), 28.

12. Oscar A. Romero, *The Violence of Love*, trans. James R. Brockman (London: Orbis, 2004), 26. I'm not suggesting that Romero's bent toward liberation theology should be embraced, only that this quote emphasizes that maltreatment of any of God's creation should correspondingly offend the church. Here Romero is emphasizing such solidarity with the ill-treated. And while liberation theology politicizes the struggle (and not without some justification), my point here is that rather than a politicized liberation theology, a theology of solidarity is more clearly required of the church.

Chapter Four

1. Paul G. Hiebert, *Cultural Anthropology* (Grand Rapids, Mich.: Baker, 1976), 25.

2. The United Kingdom created controversy when its 2001 census divided ethnicity into the following:

- White: British
- White: Irish
- White: Other
- Mixed: White and Black Caribbean
- Mixed: White and Black African
- Mixed: White and Asian
- Mixed: Other
- Asian: Indian
- Asian: Sri Lankan
- Asian: Pakistani

- Asian: Bangladeshi
- Asian: Other
- Black or Black British: Black Caribbean
- Black or Black British: Black African
- Black or Black British: Other
- Chinese or Other: Chinese
- Chinese or Other: Other

These designations were still too imprecise for many British residents.

3. *The 2006 CIA World Factbook* (Washington, D.C.: Potomac Books).

4. The term *ethnicity*, while unwieldy and imprecise, is still employed by church leadership writers to describe various cultural heritages, when the more precise term *culture* would be more appropriate. See Kathleen Garces-Foley, *Crossing the Ethnic Divide: The Multiethnic Church on a Mission* (Oxford: Oxford University Press, 2007); Mark DeYmaz, *Building a Healthy Multi-Ethnic Church: Mandate, Commitments and Practices of a Diverse Congregation* (San Francisco: Jossey-Bass, 2007); Gary L. McIntosh and Alan McMahon, *Being the Church in a Multi-Ethnic Community: Why It Matters and How It Works* (Indianapolis, Ind.: Wesleyan Publishing House, 2012).

5. William E. Thompson and Joseph V. Hickey, *Society in Focus: An Introduction to Sociology*, 5th ed. (Boston: Allyn & Bacon, 2004).

6. Those in the upper socioeconomic level are approximately 1 to 5 percent of the North American population and are characterized by power over economic, business, and political organizations and institutions.

7. Those in the upper-middle socioeconomic level represent approximately 15 percent of the North American population and are usually white-collar workers who hold graduate degrees, possessing a significant degree of flexibility and autonomy in their work.

8. Those in the lower-middle socioeconomic level are approximately 33 percent of the North American population and are usually white-collar workers with some college education. Subsequently, they have a degree of flexibility and autonomy at work, though not as much as those of the upper-middle socioeconomic strata.

9. Those in the lower-working socioeconomic level are approximately 30 percent of the North American population. Both white- and blue-collar workers, their jobs are characterized by minimum job security, inadequate pay, and worries about losing health insurance.

10. Those in the lower socioeconomic level represent 15 percent of the North American population and often go through cycles of part-time and full-time jobs. Many times they must work more than one job to provide for their needs.

11. For a chart depicting the different age ranges for each generation, see Bob Whitesel, *Preparing the Change Reaction: How to Introduce Change in Your Church* (Indianapolis, Ind.: Wesleyan Publishing House, 2007), 53.

12. See Gary L. McIntosh, *One Church, Four Generations: Understanding and Reaching All Ages in Your Church* (Grand Rapids, Mich.: Baker, 2002); and Bob Whitesel and Kent R. Hunter, *A House Divided: Bridging the Generation Gaps in Your Church* (Nashville: Abingdon, 2000).

13. The builder generation has been labeled in various ways, for instance as the "silent generation" in William Strauss and Neil Howe, *Generations: The History of America's Future, 1954 to 2069* (New York: Quill, 1992).

14. The builder generation is labeled the "greatest generation" in Tom Brokaw, *The Greatest Generation* (New York: Random House, 2004).

15. Robert Jenson, "White Privilege Shapes the US," in Paula S. Rothenberg, *White Privilege: Essential Readings on the Other Side of Racism* (New York: Worth, 2002), 103–106.

16. C. Peter Wagner, *Frontiers in Missionary Strategy* (Chicago: Moody Press, 1972), 96.

17. Regardless of the label, this practice often comes from veiled or subconscious desires to make over people to look like us. Jesus faced a similar creator complex when he jousted with the Pharisees and Sadducees who tried to make people over in their particular dress, social laws, etc. Jesus criticized them for their creator complex by saying:

- "The legal experts and the Pharisees sit on Moses' seat. Therefore, you must take care to do everything they say. But don't do what they do. For they tie together heavy packs that are impossible to carry. They put them on the shoulders of others, but are unwilling to lift a finger to move them" (Matt. 23:2–4 CEB).

- "You do away with God's word in favor of the rules handed down to you, which you pass on to others" (Mark 7:13 CEB).
- "How terrible for you legal experts too! You load people down with impossible burdens and you refuse to lift a single finger to help them" (Luke 11:46 CEB).

18. Charles Kraft, *Christianity in Culture: A Study of Dynamic Biblical Theologizing in Cross-Cultural Perspective* (Maryknoll, N.Y.: Orbis, 1979), 113.

19. Eddie Gibbs, *I Believe in Church Growth* (Grand Rapids, Mich.: Eerdmans, 1981), 120.

20. Quoted by Kathleen Garces-Foley, *Crossing the Ethnic Divide: The Multiethnic Church on a Mission* (Oxford: Oxford University Press, 2011), 64.

21. Daniel Sanchez, "Viable Models for Churches in Communities Experiencing Ethnic Transition" (paper, Fuller Theological Seminary, Pasadena, Calif., 1976).

22. Separate worship expressions make the multicultural alliance model more evangelistically effective, because it can reach nonchurchgoers who have strong connections to their cultures. Attendees pick the cultural style through which they best connect with God. The variety of worship styles makes this type of church more evangelistic because nonchurchgoers can find a style to which they are accustomed and can relate.

23. Multicultural congregations have rightly been criticized if they only offer culturally separate worship silos. See Manual Ortiz, *One New People: Models for Developing a Multiethnic Church* (Downers Grove, Ill.: InterVarsity Press, 1996). Here, however, Ortiz is not criticizing the multicultural alliance model, but rather uni-cultural models of church without blended unity events.

24. My case-study research leads me to believe that once young families have school-aged children they will switch to attending Sunday morning, because Sunday evening becomes too hectic with school starting the next morning.

25. A weekly Sunday evening unity service has helped St. Thomas' Anglican Church in Sheffield, England, become England's largest Anglican church with almost a dozen culturally distinct worship gatherings on Sunday morning. See Bob Whitesel, "St. Tom's: From Gathered to Scattered," in *The Gospel After Christendom: New Voices, New Cultures, New Expressions*, ed. Ryan Bolger (Grand Rapids, Mich.: Baker Academic, 2012), 291–302.

26. The Hebrew word for worship means to come close to God's majesty and adore him. It carries the idea of reverence, respect, and praise that results from a close encounter with a king. See Francis Brown, S. R. Driver, and Charles A. Briggs, *A Hebrew and English Lexicon of the Old Testament Based Upon the Lexicon of William Gesenius* (Oxford: Clarendon Press, 1974), 1005. Worship should not be about fellowship (the New Testament Christians had meals for that), but rather about personal communion with God. This reminds us that worship should be about connecting with God and not about creating friendships among people (we have time before and after worship for getting to know one another in fellowship halls and in common areas). Making worship into a fellowship among humans robs its place as the supernatural intersection between humans and the heavenly Father. While unity is needed, it should not be attained at the expense of worship, which is primarily intended as an environment in which to connect with God.

27. Ronald J. Sider et al., *Linking Arms, Linking Lives: How Urban-Suburban Partnerships Can Transform Communities* (Grand Rapids, Mich.: Baker, 2008).

28. External church planting should be distinguished from internal church planting. In the latter, the planted church remains part of the sponsoring church. It remains internal to the organization that helped launch it. The strategic importance of internal planting has largely been overlooked by church planting proponents, but external plants have been proposed by churches with multiple sites or campuses, which are more technically internal plants.

29. This type of mother-daughter relationship between two cultures usually devolves into a colonial relationship. For a helpful analysis of

how such relationships create a paternal culture that is narcissistic and steered by hubris, see Morris Berman, *Why America Failed: The Roots of Imperial Decline* (Hoboken, N.J.: Wiley, 2011).

30. Survivability ratios between internal plants and external plants can be inferred by comparing Ed Stetzer's research that says that 68 percent of church plants (external) survive (Ed Stetzer and Dave Travis, "Improving the Health and Survivability of New Churches: State of Church Planting USA," *Leadership Network*, October 26, 2007, http://leadnet.org/resources/download/improving_health_and_survivorability_of_new_churches_state_of_church_planting) to Warren Bird and Kristen Walter's research that says 90 percent of the new campuses (internal plants) in a multisite church survive (Warren Bird and Kristin Walters, "Multisite Is Multiplying: New Developments in the Movement's Expansion," *Leadership Network*, September 2, 2010, http://leadnet.org//resources/download/multisite_is_multiplying_new_developments_in_the_movements_expansion).

31. For examples of how creative change proponents are necessary for church survival and how they often get pushed out by the status quo in a congregation (and how to prevent this), see Bob Whitesel, *Staying Power: Why People Leave the Church Over Change and What You Can Do about It* (Nashville: Abingdon, 2002).

32. There is nothing wrong with blending services, because they create appreciation, understanding, and solidarity across cultural divides. For this very reason, the multicultural alliance model suggests regular unity services that are blended.

33. See Alejandro Portes and Rubén G. Rumbaut, *Immigrant American: A Portrait* (Los Angeles: University of California Press, 1996). They suggest that organizations comprised of selective adapters will be more harmonious.

34. See Rubén G. Rumbaut, "Sites of Belonging: Acculturation, Discrimination, and Ethnic Identity among Children of Immigrants," in *Discovering Successful Pathways in Children's Development: Mixed Methods in the Study of Childhood and Family Life*, ed. Thomas S. Weisner (Chicago: University of Chicago Press, 2005), 111–164; Kraft, *Christianity in Culture*, 113.

35. See Ken Davis, "Multicultural Church Planting Models," *Journal of Ministry and Theology* (Clarks Summit, Pa.: Spring 2003), 118. They also can be people who want their children to speak a common language (usually English).

36. To only offer blended options (as the multicultural blended church does) disconnects it from people who simply prefer their cultural style. I am not talking about people who believe their culture is superior to another, for this, I would argue, is immoral. Instead, I am only suggesting that churches appeal to more cultures if they offer worship for individual cultures along with unity worship which celebrates the uniqueness and equality among all cultures.

37. To understand the cultural adaption phenomena, it is helpful to understand three ways people adapt to other cultures. (See Rumbaut, "Sites of Belonging," 8; Gibbs, *I Believe in Church Growth*, 92; and Kraft, *Christianity in Culture*, 113.)

- Consonant adaption. These are people who readily join in with another culture. They willingly adopt other cultures and enjoy the melting pot of cultures that emerge.
- Selective adaption. These are people that partially adapt to a new culture, but not completely. They still hold some of their traditional preferences and don't want to lose them. (See Portes and Rumbaut, *Immigrant American*.)
- Dissonant adaption. These are people who adapt very little, preferring the familiarity and reassurance of their own culture. I have a friend who is an African-American, and he proudly wears his tribal *dashiki* in North America. He attends a black church where other attendees often wear this attire and he goes by his African name. I asked why he chose the church he attends and he said, "I am proud of my black heritage, and I don't want my children to forget where they are from. Attending a black church that embraces my heritage is important for me." It is this last group that the multicultural blended church poorly serves. Instead, the blended format reaches out to the consonant adapters. For partial and dissonant adapters, who dearly love and value their culture, the blended format often

does not allow them to experience enough of their personal culture, and they feel disconnected from the blended.

38. C. Peter Wagner, *Our Kind of People: The Ethical Dimensions of Church Growth in America* (Louisville: Westminster John Knox, 1979), 162.

39. Ibid., 147.

40. It is possible that Times Square Church draws multiple cultures simply because New York itself draws multiple cultures, and the church is a microcosm of that.

41. Bianca Tavera, personal conversation with author, February 10, 2012.

42. Kraft, *Christianity in Culture*, 113.

43. Robert M. Fowler, Edith Waldvogel Blumhofer, and Fernando F. Segovia, *New Paradigms for Bible Study: The Bible in the Third Millennium* (New York: T&T Clark International, 2004), 234.

Chapter Five

1. The ideal team as including approximately twelve people is defined in Bob Whitesel and Kent R. Hunter, *A House Divided: Bridging the Generation Gaps in Your Church* (Nashville: Abingdon, 2000), 26. Some researchers have observed effective small teams having as many as twenty-five participants (Jon R. Katzenbach and Douglas K. Smith, *The Wisdom of Teams: Creating the High-Performance Organization* [New York: Harper Business, 2003], 45). However, Katzenbach and Smith also found that the most common size of an effective team was approximately twelve participants (p. xvii).

2. Eric Sundstrom classifies workplace teams into several types in Eric Sundstrom and Associates, "The Challenges of Supporting Work Team Effectiveness," in *Supporting Work Team Effectiveness* (San Francisco: Jossey-Bass, 1999), 3–23. Here they have been adapted for the church context:

- Groups serving the church attendees: Bible studies, music teams, Sunday school classes, ushers, etc.

- Groups that serve nonchurchgoers: food pantry, English as a second language courses, community service teams, etc.
- Administrative groups that manage the church: boards, committees, leadership teams, etc.
- Project groups that work together on a project with a fixed time frame: special event groups, disaster response groups, Lenten groups, etc.

3. The term *small group* sometimes puts off people because they may have had some sort of small group program forced upon them. At other times, people dislike this term because they tried a small group and it wasn't the type for them. One person grumbled to me, "I've sat around somebody's living room with my shoes off singing 'Kum ba Yah' enough for a lifetime. Sitting around waiting for someone to spill their guts is not for me. I like being involved in doing. Maybe a maintenance project at the church. You get to know someone working alongside of them. That's my type of group."

4. Matthew 24:1–3.

5. Matthew 10:5–10.

6. Luke 16:13.

7. Ed Stetzer and Thom S. Rainer, *Transformational Church: Creating a New Scorecard for Congregations* (Nashville: B&H, 2010), 176–177.

8. Ibid.

9. Thom S. Rainer, "Twelve in 2012: Trends in Healthy Churches," *Thom S. Rainer* (blog) January 3, 2012, http://www.thomrainer.com/2012/01/03/twelve_in_2012_trends_in_healthy_churches_trends_7_to_12.

10. Peter Block, *Community: The Structure of Belonging* (San Francisco: Berrett-Koehler, 2008), 95.

11. Katzenbach and Smith, *Wisdom of Teams*, xxx.

12. Nancy Gallagher, *Quakers in the Israel-Palestinian Conflict: The Dilemmas of NGO Humanitarian Activism* (Cairo: American University in Cairo Press, 2007), 163.

13. Joel Comiskey, "History of the Cell Movement," accessed December 3, 2012, http://www.joelcomiskeygroup.com/articles/tutorials/cellHistory-1.html.

14. Joel Comiskey, *The Church That Multiplies: Growing a Healthy Cell Church in North America* (Edmond, Okla.: CCS Publishing, 2008).

15. Eddie Gibbs, *Body Building Exercises for the Local Church* (London: Falcon, 1979), 55.

16. John Wimber, cited in C. Peter Wagner, *Your Church Can Grow* (Glendale, Calif.: G/L Publications, 1976), 107–108.

17. Stetzer and Rainer, *Transformational Church*, 175.

18. Andy Stanley and Bill Willits, *Creating Community: 5 Keys to Building Small Group Culture* (Sisters, Ore.: Multnomah, 2004).

19. Larry Osborne, *Sticky Church* (Grand Rapids, Mich.: Zondervan, 2008); and Nelson Searcy and Kerrick Thomas, *Activate: An Entirely New Approach to Small Groups* (Ventura, Calif.: Regal, 2008).

20. Kent Hunter, *Heart-to-Heart Groups* (Corunna, Ind.: Church Growth Center, 1990).

21. The definition of regular attendance is subjective, and for this discussion it will be left to the discretion of the individual church.

22. Lyle E. Schaller, *Growing Plans: Strategies to Increase Your Church's Membership* (Nashville: Abingdon, 1983), 26.

23. Mike Breen and Bob Hopkins, *Clusters: Creative Mid-Sized Missional Communities* (Sheffield, UK: Anglican Church Planting Initiatives, 2008).

24. Whitesel and Hunter, *House Divided*, 26–27.

25. The Dunbar number is a sociological phenomena whereby people feel most comfortable in an extended community of less than 150 people. Kevin Martin in *The Myth of the 200 Barrier* ([Nashville: Abingdon, 2005], 42), says, "Whenever a service or group exceeds 150 members, problems or tension will develop." See also Robin Dunbar, interview by Rachel Martin, *All Things Considered*, NPR, June 5, 2011.

26. Mike Breen in Bob Whitesel, *Inside the Organic Church: Learning from 12 Emerging Congregations* (Nashville: Abingdon, 2006), 5–6.

27. Often administrative committees have been populated with the same people for so long that they have developed a committed friendship in addition to a commitment to a task. When this happens, a church board or committee has actually become a heart-to-heart group.

28. Kelly O'Donnell, "On Leadership and Teamwork: A Narrative and a Model," *Journal of Psychology and Theology* 39, no. 1 (2011): 73.

29. Ibid., 73–74.

30. Lencioni added commitment and accountability as the fourth and fifth elements of a healthy team. In my view these are the sub-sets of trust in Lencioni's model. Thus in the four-heart model, these elements are incorporated within several of the other hearts.

31. Patrick Lencioni, *The Five Dysfunctions of a Team: A Leadership Fable* (San Francisco: Jossey-Bass, 2002), 195.

32. Ibid., 212.

33. As noted in the introduction, this statement is the essence of the *missio Dei*, indicating our loving heavenly Creator is seeking, much like a father would, to reconnect with all of his offspring, even the wayward ones. When churches effectively participate in this mission, they are sometimes called missional congregations.

34. Because of the overriding nature and eternal destiny tied to this mission, accountability to God and one another comes in this missional model before discussion or conflict and results. No fruitful discussion, useful conflict resolution, or rewarding outcome occurs in a team that is not first accountable to God and his Word.

35. Lencioni, *Five Dysfunctions of a Team*, 202.

36. John Wesley, "Notes on the Bible," Bible Suite, accessed December 3, 2012, http://wes.biblecommenter.com/proverbs/27.htm.

37. Lencioni, *Five Dysfunctions of a Team*, 216.

38. Ibid., 195.

39. Katzenbach and Smith, *Wisdom of Teams*, 12. Too often groups are formed just for the sake of fellowship. Katzenbach and Smith warn that this is a mistake. A small group must set its sights upon some tangible results that the group can accomplish. They say, "Performance, however, is the primary objective, while a team remains the means, not the end" (p. 12).

Chapter Six

1. Ralph P. Martin, *Worship in the Early Church* (Grand Rapids, Mich.: Eerdmans, 1964), 10.

2. For more on how the Hebrew and Greek words for *worship* convey a personal and arduous emphasis, see J. S. McEwen, "Worship," in *A Theological Word Book of the Bible*, ed. Alan Richardson (New York: Macmillan, 1950), 287–289.

3. Ibid. The most common Old Testament word is *hishtahawah* which is derived from *shaha*.

4. Ibid., 287.

5. Ibid.; see also Martin, *Worship in the Early Church*, 10–12.

6. Martin describes the two biblical words for worship (*bowing down* and *service*) as "the two prominent terms which throw light on the underlying principles of worship." See *Worship in the Early Church*, 11.

7. Fasting is mentioned here in conjunction with worship, and Everett Harrison observes that this underscores their need for guidance. Harrison also notes that while some translations render this "while they were ministering to the Lord," it should more accurately thought of as worshiping. See Everett F. Harrison, *Acts: The Expanding Church* (Chicago: Moody Press, 1975), 203.

8. McEwen, "Worship," 287.

9. Quoted by John W. Howe and Sam C. Pascoe, *Our Anglican Heritage*, 2nd ed. (Eugene, Ore.: Wipf & Stock, 2010), 41.

10. One wouldn't visit an emperor or king without preparation. Therefore, it should not seem unusual that the words for *worship* found in the Old and New Testaments are also synonymous with *service* and *labor*. J. S. McEwen points out that the great preparation the Jews of the Old Testament put into worship was precisely because they didn't want worship to become empty ceremonialism. The book of Psalms testifies to how the Jewish priests, musicians, and choirs worked hard to ensure that, though preparation was necessary, worship remained an encounter and their planning never overshadowed worship's heavenward connection. McEwen, "Worship," 288.

11. J. S. McEwen stated, "The inward spiritual attitude of the worshiper thus begins to come to the front as an important factor in worship." McEwen, "Worship," 287.

12. For a fuller examination of the missional task, see Bob White-sel, *Organix: Signs of Leadership in a Changing Church* (Nashville: Abingdon, 2011), 9–10.

13. J. S. McEwen states that when the Bible attaches service to worship, it conveys the idea that all service to God is in some respect worship. McEwen writes, "Since worship means the service of God, and this in turn implies loving one's neighbour, it follows that every kindly act performed in this spirit and intention is an act of worship" (McEwen, "Worship," 288–289). While this is true, this chapter is primarily concerned with the importance of worship as a drawing near to God in adoration, humility, service, and transformation.

14. Martin, *Worship in the Early Church*, 13.

15. Rudolph Otto, *The Idea of the Holy*, trans. John W. Harvey (Oxford: Oxford University Press, 1958), 52. Rudolph Otto suggested a helpful depiction of God's duality of holiness and approachability that can be understood by thinking of God's holiness as *tremendum* (awe-inspiring) and *fascinans* (captivating) in both attractiveness (to him) and repulsiveness (from him, because of our sin) (p. 52).

16. Martin, *Worship in the Early Church*, 14.

17. Many scholars believe it is fruitless to draw categorical distinctions between "psalms, hymns and spiritual songs" as mentioned in Colossians 3:16 and Ephesians 5:19–20. This is because these words do not suggest categories, but rather allude to the rich variety of worship expressions in the early church. See Martin, *Worship in the Early Church*, 47–48.

18. Here the KJV may hold a bit more accuracy according to Ralph Martin, for James' admonition most likely refers to Davidic psalms. See Martin, *Worship in the Early Church*, 43.

19. Harrison, *Acts*, 203.

20. Martin, *Worship in the Early Church*, 15.

21. Quoted by Ben Witherington III, *We Have Seen His Glory: A Vision of Kingdom Worship* (Grand Rapids, Mich.: Eerdmans, 2010), 28.

22. Charlton T. Lewis et al., *A Latin Dictionary Founded on Andrews' Edition of Freund's Latin Dictionary* (Oxford: Clarendon, 1996), 112.

23. Whitesel, *Organix*, 121–137.

24. Kent R. Hunter, "The Quality Side of Church Growth," in *Church Growth State of the Art*, ed. C. Peter Wagner (Carol Stream, Ill.: Tyndale, 1986), 79.

25. Kent R. Hunter, personal conversation with author, April 2005.

26. Charles Kraft reminds us that Christianity is "supra-cultural." By this he means that Christianity is not a culture, but rather principles and powers that are higher than culture, and thus can permeate all cultures. See Charles H. Kraft, *Christianity in Culture: A Study in Dynamic Biblical Theologizing in Cross-Cultural Perspective* (Maryknoll, N.Y.: Orbis, 1979), 116–146.

27. Hunter, "Quality Side," 79.

28. The worship leader must not simply adopt all elements of a culture, for while some elements may not run counter to the teachings of Christ, other elements will. Eddie Gibbs offers the helpful metaphor of sifting a culture, meaning that leaders must separate out elements that run counter to the good news. See Eddie Gibbs, *I Believe in Church Growth* (Grand Rapids, Mich.: Eerdmans, 1981), 120.

29. I have discussed at length why worship is not the best place to bring about reconciliation in Whitesel, *Organix*, 59–82. Because worship is an intimate encounter with God, it is misdirected if it is tasked with bringing about cross-cultural understanding (at least for this discussion). Cross-cultural understanding (and reconciliation) is better served by concerts instead of worship, equal partnerships instead of separate congregations, and diversity in leadership instead of oligarchies.

30. For more on the Quaker liturgy that emphasizes leading by the Holy Spirit rather than by configuration, see John Punshon, "An Experience of Unprogrammed Worship" and "Starting to Worship Without Words," in *Encounter with Silence: Reflections from the Quaker Tradition* (Richmond, Ind.: Friends United Press, 1987), 21–100.

31. The basics of how a church can learn improvisation in worship for more healthy spiritual encounter can be found in Bob Whitesel, "Learn to Improv," in *Inside the Organic Church: Learning from 12 Emerging Congregations* (Nashville: Abingdon, 2006), 119–122.

32. Such participation by laity in the worship service is customary in many small churches due to lack of paid staff. I have observed that this is a strength of such smaller churches (see Whitesel, *Organix*, 53–54). However, once churches begin to run over one hundred attendees, I have noticed that lay leadership in worship drops quickly. This exercise is designed to help keep lay involvement integral to the worship service because laity can provide a helpful view of how worship is impacting lives.

Chapter Seven

1. This illustration—as well as all narratives that begin each chapter—are drawn from combining real-life experiences of client churches to create a scenario that helps the reader grasp the insights of the chapter. However, to my knowledge the use of eminent domain by a municipality to take a church building has not yet occurred, though there are signs that courts are increasingly looking at this possibility. For example, courts have already permitted municipalities to seize personal property under eminent domain rationale for a commercial development (see Kelo v. City of New London, 125 S. Ct. 2655 [2005]), and courts have permitted a municipality to use eminent domain to seize undeveloped land owned by a church (see Faith Temple Church v. Town of Brighton, 794 N.Y.S. 2d 249 [4th Dept. 2005]).

2. Bob Whitesel, *Organix: Signs of Leadership in a Changing World* (Nashville: Abingdon, 2011), 9–10.

3. I have written two books on how spiritual transformation takes place in a similar manner to a journey. For more on how Christians can navigate their spiritual journey as well as help others, see Bob Whitesel, *Spiritual Waypoints: Helping Other Navigate the Journey* (Indianapolis, Ind.: Wesleyan Publishing House, 2010); and Bob Whitesel, *Waypoint: Navigating Your Spiritual Journey* (Indianapolis, Ind.: Wesleyan Publishing House, 2010).

4. There are hundreds of terms utilized to describe congregations. This list is only the most basic, using labels that are widely employed or have historical significance. Also note that these appellations are not

self-excluding because several designations can be used to describe the same congregation.

5. For a good overview of the split between congregations with a traditional emphasis and numerous upstart denominations, see Roger Finke and Rodney Stark, "How the Upstart Sects Won America: 1776–1850," *Journal for the Scientific Study of Religion*, no. 28 (1989): 27–44; and Roger Finke and Rodney Stark, *The Churching of America 1776–2005: Winners and Losers in Our Religious Economy* (Piscataway, N.J.: Rutgers University Press, 2005).

6. For a good overview of the inception of the Holiness Movement, see Douglas A. Sweeney, *The American Evangelical Story: A History of the Movement* (Grand Rapids, Mich.: Baker Academic, 2005), 133–154.

7. Social gospel churches embrace much more than just meeting the needs of the poor, but it is their healing of the hurts of society that is appropriate for this discussion. For more on this viewpoint, see Walter Rauschenbusch, *A Theology for the Social Gospel* (Louisville: Westminster John Knox, 1917).

8. Vinson Synan, *The Holiness-Pentecostal Tradition: Charismatic Movements in the Twentieth Century* (Grand Rapids, Mich.: Eerdmans, 1997).

9. David Allan Hubbard, *What We Evangelicals Believe* (Pasadena, Calif.: Fuller Seminary Press, 1991).

10. These were in fact Jesus' last earthly words. Immediately afterwards, "He was lifted up and a cloud took him out of their sight" (Acts 1:9 CEB). What would these last instructions be? What would he choose as the last phrase that would resonate with his hearers? Acts 1:8 gives us the answer.

11. This is not to suggest that needs in developing countries should be ignored, only that there should be a balance in a church's ministry between those nearby and those far away.

12. See the beginnings of Robertson's concepts of this in Roland Robertson, *Globalization: Social Theory and Global Culture* (Thousand Oaks, Calif.: Sage Publications, 1992). His more-developed ideas can be found in "The Conceptual Promise of Glocalization: Commonality and Diversity" (Seoul: Proceedings of the International Forum on Cultural Diversity and Common Values, 2003), 76–89.

13. See Bob Roberts, *Glocalization: How Followers of Jesus Engage a Flat World* (Grand Rapids, Mich.: Zondervan, 2007); and Tormod Engelsviken, Erling Lundeby, and Dagfinn Solheim, eds., *The Church Going Glocal: Mission and Globalisation* (Eugene, Ore.: Wipf & Stock, 2011).

14. Though Roberts attempts to depict glocalization as a meeting of believers and nonbelievers needs, his emphasis in his book *Glocalization* focuses heavily upon meeting the needs of the unchurched (pp. 28–29). While this is the primary purpose of the good news, by unintentionally downplaying the parallel needs of the congregation, many churches burn out their volunteers in efforts directed outward and not inward too.

15. Even though a local church may be physically bound by its neighborhood, Christ intended the church to have influence and persuasion beyond its locale (see Acts 1:8; Luke 24:47; and Isa. 49:6).

16. C. Peter Wagner, *Church Growth and the Whole Gospel: A Biblical Mandate* (San Francisco: Harper & Row, 1981), 52.

17. Samuel L. Gaertner and John F. Dovidio, "Toward the Elimination of Racism: The Study of Intergroup Behavior," in *Bigotry, Prejudice and Hatred: Definitions, Causes & Solutions*, eds. Robert M. Baird and Stuart E. Rosenbaum, 2nd ed. (Amherst, N.Y.: Prometheus, 1999), 245–250.

18. Hannah Gray, "The DecAid Project Established," *The Sojourn*, February 1, 2012. See also http://www.decaidproject.org.

19. See the stories of this in Ronald J. Sider et al., *Linking Arms, Linking Lives: How Urban-Suburban Partnerships Can Transform Communities* (Grand Rapids, Mich.: Baker, 2008).

Chapter Eight

1. See A. D. Nock, *Conversion: The Old and the New in Religion from Alexander the Great to Augustine of Hippo* (Baltimore: John Hopkins University Press, 1933); and Flo Conway and Jim Siegelman, *Snapping: America's Epidemic of Sudden Personality Change*, 2nd ed. (New York: Stillpoint, 1995).

2. See Robert Jay Lifton, *Thought Reform and the Psychology of Totalism: A Study of Brainwashing in China* (New York: Norton, 1961).

3. "Conversion," *Google*, March 20, 2012, https://www.google.com/search?hl=en&source=hp&biw=&bih=&q=conversion&gbv=2&oq=conversion&gs_l=heirloom-hp.3..0l10.1024.1986.0.2149.10.8.0.2.2.0.96.570.8.8.0...0.0...1c.1.hb-gMENBjuE.

4. Richard Peace, "Conflicting Understandings of Christian Conversion: A Missiological Challenge," *International Bulletin of Missionary Research*, 28, no. 1 (2004): 8.

5. William F. Arndt and F. Wilbur Gingrich, trans., *A Greek-English Lexicon of the New Testament and Other Early Literature* (Chicago: University of Chicago Press, 1957), 513.

6. Peace, "Conflicting Understandings," 8.

7. This is only a partial list of the spiritual waypoints. For more on the waypoints model and how people make a spiritual decision that results in new life, see Bob Whitesel, *Spiritual Waypoints: Helping Others Navigate the Journey* (Indianapolis, Ind.: Wesleyan Publishing House, 2010); and Bob Whitesel, *Waypoint: Navigating Your Spiritual Journey* (Indianapolis, Ind.: Wesleyan Publishing House, 2010).

8. Arndt and Gingrich, *Greek-English Lexicon*, 668–670.

9. Robert E. Coleman, *The Heart of the Gospel: The Theology Behind the Master Plan of Evangelism* (Grand Rapids, Mich.: Baker, 2011), 160.

10. Arndt and Gingrich, *Greek-English Lexicon*, 668–670.

11. Ibid., 301.

12. Peace, "Conflicting Understandings," 8.

13. For a helpful comparison of the differences between sudden conversion and gradual conversion, see Whitesel, *Spiritual Waypoints*, 142. There you will find an explanation why some researchers have found that only about 10 percent of the sudden conversions result in long-term changes in personal behavior (Donald Miller, *Reinventing American Protestantism: Christianity in the New Millennium* [Berkley: University of California Press, 1997], 171–172). For an illustration of how this transformation takes place, see the story of Oksana, a fictional story of transformation, woven throughout Whitesel, *Waypoints*.

14. Richard Peace, *Conversion in the New Testament: Paul and the Twelve* (Grand Rapids, Mich.: Eerdmans, 1999), 4.

15. Peace, "Conflicting Understandings," 8–9. See also Charles Kraft, "Christian Conversion as a Dynamic Process," in *International Christian Broadcasters Bulletin*, 2nd qtr. (Colorado Springs: International Christian Broadcasters, 1974).

16. Richard Peace states, "What Mark sought to communicate in his gospel was the process by which these twelve men gradually turned, over time, from their culturally derived understanding of Jesus as a great teacher to the amazing discovery that he was actually the Messiah who was the Son of God. In showing how the Twelve turned to Jesus, step-by-step, Mark was inviting his readers to undergo the same journey of conversion" (Peace, *Conversion in the New Testament*, 4).

17. Scot McKnight, *Turning to Jesus: The Sociology of Conversion in the Gospels* (Louisville: Westminster John Knox, 2002), 5.

18. I have stated, "The evangelical church may be limiting the number of wayfarers she can help by focusing too exclusively on sudden conversion" (Whitesel, *Spiritual Waypoints*, 138).

19. Lewis R. Rambo, *Understanding Religious Conversion* (New Haven, Conn.: Yale University Press, 1993), 165.

20. This change in nomenclature for labeling this section is necessitated because, as we have seen in this chapter, new life is a supernatural intersection that only God can create.

21. Peace, "Conflicting Understandings," 8.

22. I have adapted these questions from these sources: James F. Engel and Wilbert Norton, *What's Gone Wrong With the Harvest?: A Communication Strategy for World Evangelism* (Grand Rapids, Mich.: Zondervan, 1975), 45; James F. Engel, *Contemporary Christian Communications: Its Theory and Practice* (Nashville: Thomas Nelson, 1979), 63–87, 225; James F. Engel and William A. Dyrness, *Changing the Mind of Missions: Where Have We Gone Wrong?* (Downers Grove, Ill.: InterVarsity Press, 2000), 100–101.

Chapter Nine

1. The exercises in this book are attributed to the colleagues, students, and researchers who submitted them. Since many exercises are derivative of similar and/or earlier exercises, no effort has been

made to cite the originator. This should not be taken as an effort to take away credit from the initiator.

2. The impact exercises are often more numerous because there are so many different congregational situations and trajectories that more impact exercises are needed to allow for greater customization to your local context.

3. As you read the exercises, you probably noticed a number of common threads emerging. These are general ideas that can be found running through all of the exercises in each chapter. For example, a common thread running through the exercises submitted for multicultural fellowship (chapter 4) is that congregants must personally (face-to-face and heart-to-heart) encounter people who are unlike them. Thus, a common thread in that chapter is getting people in your congregation fellowshipping and meeting people who are not like them. Having a sense of the common threads can also help you customize or improvise your own exercises from the examples in this book.

4. This has also been called the principle of "Yes, and . . ." For example, in this narrative instead of blocking the action you might say, "Yes, you are a tree, and . . . there is a bird in it."

5. Tory Helgeson, personal conversation with author, April 2010.

6. For more on accepting (the "Yes, and . . ." principle) and blocking (the opposite maneuver), see Keith Johnstone, *Impro: Improvisation and the Theatre* (New York: Routledge, 1989), 94–100.

Is there a cure for what ails the common church?

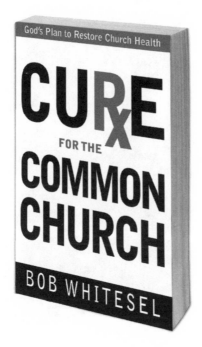

God's answer begins with you. Something is not quite right in the local church. Many Christians see the symptoms of decline in fellowship and spiritual vitality. If health and life are indications of growth, their congregation is not well. Unfortunately, the ailing church is becoming the common church.

Professor and church-growth consultant Bob Whitesel has written *Cure for the Common Church* to offer potent and proven cures to foster health in their local congregations. By thoughtfully examining Scriptures, he applies truths through real-life experience from his years of consulting. Questions for group study also help members explore and discern together how to become a healthy force in their church.

Cure for the Common Church
ISBN: 978-0-89827-587-2

wesleyan
publishing
house

www.wesleyan.org/wph
1.800.493.7539

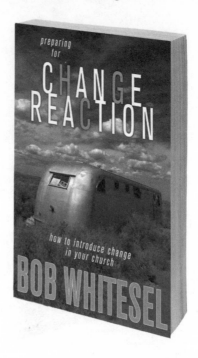